How to Talk

Nashville

How to Talk
Nashville

A Cross-Cultural Guide for
Newcomers to the American South

MARK BLEVINS

Modern Piddler Publishing
Nashville

HOW TO TALK NASHVILLE: A CROSS-CULTURAL GUIDE
FOR NEWCOMERS TO THE AMERICAN SOUTH.
Copyright © 2015 by Mark Blevins. All rights reserved.

Developmental Editor: EMILY BLEVINS

Editor: MARK A. BILBREY

Cover design by CARRIE SUBLETT

Interior design by 52 Novels.

For information, address MODERN PIDDLER PUBLISHING
at P.O. Box 60063, Nashville, TN 37206 or
email modernpiddler@howtotalknashville.com.

FIRST EDITION

ISBN: 978-0-9969752-0-9

Printed in the U.S.A.

For Patrick Crouch, whose encouragement and fiery spirit are never forgotten.

Culture is communication and communication is culture.
— Edward T. Hall, *The Silent Language*

Contents

CHAPTER ONE

Nashville, We Have a Problem

There's a collective insecurity among many from the American South that people from other parts of the country and world believe us to be an uneducated, illogical, and self-defeating lot—or, to use a word well known to Southerners, *backward*.

Pop culture has long portrayed Southern life as built around the triple pillars of pick-up trucks, fried chicken, and moonshine-fueled hoedowns. And just as the tired, hick-invoking banjo melody from *Deliverance* was falling out of popular memory, a raft of reality TV programs arrived to reinforce and preserve those stereotypes for a new generation.

Naturally, Southerners have plenty of their own misleading ideas about regional cultures, the "Yankee" thing being most prominent. Yankees might stereotype Southerners as country bumpkins living in dirt-floored shacks and enjoying the right to carry guns in bars and playgrounds, while

Southerners stereotype Yankees as sociopathic day traders hell-bent on destroying the world's financial system for selfish gain.

Yankees accuse Southerners of being superficial and inefficient. Meanwhile, Southerners find Yankees to be ill-mannered and consider Yankee ambition morally suspect.

Yanks say Southerners have bad schools, and Southerners counter that Yankees have bad weather.

This sort of inter-cultural mud-slinging is probably not the pathway to societal harmony, nor is it likely to produce good communication between the people of these regions. As more people from around the country and world come to the American South to live, work or vacation, the need to improve cross-cultural relations becomes more apparent. Good communication is at the heart of this and can be improved by understanding *where someone is coming from* and not just where they're from.

Life in the changing South can be made a great deal more enjoyable (and intelligible) if we move beyond stereotyping and begin to see the actual dynamics driving behavior. Each passing exchange at the grocery that ends in awkwardness, every misperceived slight at work that leads to hard feelings, and all the dumbfounded expressions at Nashville's honky-tonks serve to diminish us all.

Some things need to be explained.

Nashville is a crossroads town.

Early frontiersmen could pass through the Cumberland Gap, float down the Cumberland River and come to what is now Nashville, where the Natchez Trace led to the land of deltas and rich hunting grounds of the Deep South. Native Americans used these routes for millennia to hunt and trade between the Mississippi Delta and Appalachian Mountains. Before that, big game like bison and deer carved the ancient highways out of dense forests on their migratory journeys toward the life-sustaining salt licks of pre-Nashville.

These routes have a long history and made this city an early gateway into the South. In many ways, it remains so today.

When WSM 650 AM first broadcast its 50,000-watt clear channel transmission in 1932, the beacon of country music was heard from coast to coast. Americans everywhere could listen to the mash-up of folk music that filtered from all points Southern to the stage of the Grand Ole Opry and back out through the ether. If you followed that beacon, you found yourself in Nashville. If you thought of Nashville, you thought of those country songs. Nashville would become a major conduit through which others understood Southern culture.

Country music has grown to become a powerhouse in the entertainment industry and continues to be both beacon and ambassador of the South. No doubt this makes some Southerners cringe, as many don't see themselves or their culture represented in country music. To put it simply, not everyone is the same, and the South can't be described by any one set of characteristics. The South is many things to many different kinds of people. Nashville isn't the same as New Orleans. Jackson, Mississippi isn't like Boone, North Carolina. East Texas isn't like North Florida. There are many different flavors of Southern in the American South. Yet there exists something distinctive and unifying about Southern culture. It isn't the music, or the *ain'ts* and *y'alls*. Nor is it a love of pickup trucks or fried chicken or moonshine-fueled hoedowns (though the author recommends all of these).

The unifying principle of the South is the cultural perspective of its people, one that leads to a communication style that is unique in the United States. It's here that we find the source of many "cross-cultural" misunderstandings.

It causes no small amount of discomfort to suggest the South has a culture separate from the rest of the country— ultimately, we are all Americans with a larger culture in common. However, there is something fundamentally different about the South, and the language and tools of the social sciences are well suited to compare regional subcultures within the U.S. In doing so, we gain both a framework to describe the South's unique culture and strategies to better engage the Southern perspective. Southerners, too, will find insight into their own communication style as well as that of other Americans.

Newcomers would be well advised to respect Southern ways, though this is just good policy for any outsider traveling or moving to a new culture. And there's the rub. The American South *is American,* so many newcomers are slow to understand how different it can be. The highway signs and TV shows may be the same, but the culture remains fundamentally distinctive.

The U.S. is a big place with definable regions. We associate certain characteristics with the people of these regions and can identify some of the historical or environmental factors that fostered them—the fast-talking Yankee, the rugged Northwesterner, the earnest Midwesterner, the free-spirited Californian. These stereotypical traits don't really tell us much about an individual, but nonetheless, we all use them as shortcuts to explain the unknown.

We would do better to use an *archetypical* model, understanding individuals are quite varied but that their culture can produce a commonly occurring set of characteristics. Some individuals represent these archetypes precisely, while others represent various degrees of these traits or none at all. To find the Southern archetype, we must understand the culture that produces it.

In many ways, the Southerner can be explained simply as another regional version of American, born of a unique set of historical and geographical circumstances. Our mother cultures, immigrant experiences, New World adaptation, and historical developments have led each American subculture to its present state. So it's in these places we'll search for a *fundamental distinction* in the communication behavior of Southern culture. To find this distinction, we'll use the tools of cross-culturalists and focus them on the South.

First, however, we must open our minds and recognize how our own culture both informs and inhibits our understanding of the world. Cross-cultural research is a relatively new field of study, but the problems it is meant to solve are as old as humanity. Four hundred years ago, a European philosopher succinctly identified our ongoing dilemma:

> [People] … are tormented with the opinions they have of things and not by the things themselves. It [would be] a great victory obtained for the relief of our miserable human condition, could this proposition be established for certain and true throughout.
>
> – Michel de Montaigne, 1580[1]

Twentieth-century philosopher and funkmaster George Clinton put it another way: "Free your mind, and your ass will follow." Clinton seems to implore us to free our minds of "the opinions [we] have of things." Where do these opinions come from? Montaigne, the oft-called father of skepticism, suggests our opinions have not been independently examined, just adopted. It's as though the opinions pre-date the individual. If the "tormented" would only evaluate "things" for themselves, they might find relief from the pre-existing ideas that come, inevitably, from culture. We have something in common with the tormented people Montaigne observed centuries ago—indeed, with all of humanity: our beliefs, customs, values, and ideas have been handed down and seem to us like part of the natural order.

We look through the prism of our culture and witness the world through its lens. Through its language, we describe and give meaning to everything we experience. With our collected systems of ideas and values, we determine what is good and bad, what is preferred and not preferred.

If culture provides the way to understand our world, it also limits us. The prism through which we see out distorts the light as it passes through, altering the image. Our words and language fall short in describing new experiences and ideas. Our value systems become inflexible and outgrown by historical and social developments.

"We think our minds are free ... but we have been thoroughly brainwashed," writes cross-culturalist Richard D. Lewis. "Collective programming in our culture, begun in the cradle and reinforced in kindergarten, school and the workplace, convinces us that we are normal, others eccentric."[2] This process of socialization is known as *cultural conditioning*. The Peace Corps, whose work is based on cross-cultural exchange, explains it like this:

> [Cultural conditioning] goes on in all cultures, but the specific behaviors that people acquire, the precise content of their conditioning, varies considerably from group to group. [While] it is behaviors that people learn through this process, they are automatically learning and internalizing the values and beliefs behind those behaviors.[3]

In many places across the globe, proper dining etiquette means eating with your hands from shared, communal dishes. Typically, these cultures have strong customs regarding hand washing and dining technique, so members must learn these specific customs in order to behave in a socially acceptable way. But beyond learning good table manners, members of these cultures are learning something about the group to which they belong—they affirm

7

their interconnectedness by coming together and sharing the same dish. The learned behavior is the style of cooking and eating; the learned values and beliefs are related to group cohesion and communal survival. From their perspective, eating a breakfast biscuit in a car while driving to work might be enormously disconcerting, just as having a dinner guest put their hand in a bowl of peas would freak out most Westerners.

Human behaviors are made right or wrong by the defining power of culture and the conditioning of its people—we all come by our ways and beliefs honestly. Our goal in this cross-cultural study of the American South is to find the values and motivations *hidden behind* the behavior, and thereby understand Southerners themselves.

Nashville, like the South as a whole, is rebirthing itself. This is not a unique development, and proclamations of a "new South" have been heard many times before. But today, people are moving into this region instead of out. Migration rates to the South from other regions within the U.S. continue to be the highest in the nation as sunnier climes and growing business environments beckon those from all over.[4] The South, Midwest, and Northeast had roughly equal populations in the 1950s. Now the South nearly equals the Midwest and Northeast combined.[5] And it boasts the largest economic GDP of any U.S. region.[6]

As these changes are taking place, Southern culture seems to be enjoying something of a renaissance, or at least to have become a media darling. But country music,

Southern hip hop, and New Orleans jazz are only part of the South's constantly evolving musical heritage—just as fried chicken, moonshine, and Moon Pies are only a few of the region's culinary offerings. The multitude of cultural riches available are beyond the scope of this book.

Here we seek a general, archetypical Southern perspective that threads the history and heart of Southern culture, producing a style of communication unique among U.S. regions. Our mission is to identify this communication style, examine how it works, and explore strategies along the way that can improve cross-cultural interactions.

To accomplish this mission, we'll use the tools and language of the social sciences. History, sociology, psychology, and anthropology have long sought to understand the complexities of cultures. As these fields have developed, cross-pollinated, and been reshaped into multidisciplinary endeavors, many ways of explaining human behavior have been discovered and explored. This little book doesn't aim to encompass these many worthwhile and enlightening directions of thought. Rather, the purpose here is to employ these important works to describe the nature of Southern and non-Southern communication behavior, with the ultimate goal of helping to bridge a cultural divide that predates English immigration to America.

CHAPTER TWO

How's Your Mama and Them?

A couple sits in a thinly populated New Orleans bar early in the afternoon. The doors are all open, letting in a light breeze and the gentle sounds of Bourbon Street between parties. They are first-time tourists from Los Angeles, and their presence has the blissed-out quality of recently converted cult members, all smiles and unfolding revelation.

The wife is having her hair braided by a kind gay man who considers this neighborhood bar his favorite place for drinks and socializing. She hasn't had her hair braided since she was a teenager and never in the tight, cornrow fashion more likely found on the heads of local schoolchildren. This has produced a look of amazed joy across her face. Some of the neighbors are there. Two of them have brought their dogs, which are said to be best friends that meet at this communal spot every day. The bartender is still waking up. Among the six or seven patrons are a couple of Nashvillians.

"Is everyone in the South this friendly?" the wife asks the Tennesseans who have joined in the small group's conversation.

"Maybe not *this* friendly," one of them answers, referring to the pleasant scene. "Friendliness is probably the social standard, though we have some mean ones down here too."

She sighs and appears less than blissful for the first time. "Tomorrow we return to Mordor, and I really don't want to go."

"Mordor?" (*Lord of the Rings* reigned as king of the screens at this time.)

"That's how we've come to think of L.A.," the husband explains wistfully. "We've been there twenty years and would leave in a heartbeat if we could, without looking back. We've been here a week and already feel connected to the people we've met. You can tell it's a real community. Everyone is so *welcoming* and just so... *friendly!*"

Friendliness is one of the charming characteristics many newcomers find down South. Some embrace it and some don't know quite what to do with it. Some see it as weak, or even disingenuous.

A few years ago, a Detroit native moved to Nashville to start a new life with her Southern husband. She's a strong woman, with well-defined ideas about the world and a propensity to defend them by speaking out. Upon moving down and meeting her husband's circle of friends, she immediately felt the embrace of that community.

"Everyone was so friendly and open, and it seemed like I had a group of friends waiting on me when I arrived," she recalled. It was a breath of fresh air and very different from her social situation in Detroit. Of course she had friends back home, but the social landscape down here was strikingly expansive and connected many people. In Detroit, relationships were often discarded if interests changed or things went sour. In Nashville, it seemed her husband had dozens of companions he'd collected over decades who considered their friendships to be important and enduring. Their personal histories were interwoven and their relationships were long developed. It was a bit overwhelming, but she set out to establish her place within this circle.

"There were so many people—friends of my husband—welcoming me in all kinds of friendly, generous ways," she explained. "I really jumped in with both feet and felt a sort of unconditional love I assumed was an extension of the love for my husband but genuinely given to me too." She wanted to return that generosity and be a good friend, as is her nature. She wanted to be part of the community, and she was. For the first year or so, she lived inside this charming Southern bubble. She didn't understand it all. She missed her hometown at times. But she was happy to be forging this new life down south.

One of the first hurdles she faced was in regular conversation. She was never shy, but as she became more comfortable within the group and fully joined in discussions on any topic, an awkward phenomenon emerged. Too often for her to ignore, what would begin as a rousing conversation would end as a long monologue delivered by herself. She didn't understand the problem, but it left her feeling lost and embarrassed. Unfortunately, this scenario was repeated many times.

So what was it? At first, she suspected the South didn't accept strong women and instead preferred the quiet, deferential type. But this didn't seem to be especially true for the other women in the group, so she considered the possibility that her point of view was too politically liberal for the famously conservative South. But this was East Nashville—an enclave of musicians, artists, and craft beer bohemians. Most all of her husband's friends could easily be described as politically "liberal." Was she just smarter than everyone here? It seemed they couldn't keep up with her in conversation.

It wasn't long before she was made to understand the problem with her conversational style: she was a cross-talker. An interrupter of conversation. Someone who would talk over anyone at any time. Someone who began expressing her thoughts before her conversational partners stopped expressing theirs, which for her was a perfectly acceptable way of interacting. Back home, cross-talking was not only normal—it was a sign the conversation was going well. It showed engagement and interest. But in the South, it's usually perceived as a disrespectful attempt to dominate the discussion. Typically, Southerners don't interrupt others while they're talking, and those who do are considered ill mannered. Everyone should have a right to speak their own mind, the Southern premise goes, but there are time and place restrictions on this right. Though she understood the problem, she couldn't accept it or save herself from her own cultural norm, where cross-talking is understood as a positive quality.

This began her love/hate relationship with Nashville, though cross-talking wasn't her only cultural stumbling block. She sought more intimate connections within the group but often found her efforts unsuccessful. Soon, she began to feel left out of the inner, more intimate circles within the group. The love she was greeted with upon arriving in town began to feel shallow, even insincere.

What was this Southern friendliness that once seemed so simple and unconditional but was revealed to be complex and bound by a thousand unspoken rules? She was always warmly welcomed at social gatherings, but the promise of that first year was only slowly, and partially, realized. A few years after she arrived, and after much consternation, she discovered her truly intimate friendships. Some were in that group of friends and some were not.

While the Detroit native was always considered to be inside the sphere of her husband's friend group (she married into it and found genuine friendships there), some newcomers find themselves excluded or ejected from a social circle.

A Long Islander moved to Atlanta for a new job and the next chapter of his life. Sam was excited about his prospects down South and heartily welcomed by neighbors and coworkers. His arrival and first few months were filled with nothing but promise. He accepted invitations to social gatherings and even found a place for himself at the local pub. But as time went by, he began to experience something odd: he felt lonely despite being surrounded by friendly people. He just wasn't making deeper, more satisfying kinds of friendships, and none seemed to develop past the initial, superficial phase of acquaintanceship.

However, Sam persisted and eventually made more intimate connections with a group of friends. After his period of loneliness, the feeling of developing real relationships and finding his own place was more than gratifying—it felt like a victory, and a hard won victory at that. He came to enjoy his life and to care deeply for his new friends.

When a member of this friend group—Wayne—began dating someone he considered a bad match, Sam felt compelled to voice his objection. Though he wrestled with it, he decided the right thing to do by his new friend was to share his concerns directly. Wayne brushed it off the first time it was mentioned, but when the topic arose again, he became annoyed at the meddling and told Sam to butt out. However, Sam couldn't help himself and pursued it further by discussing his objections with others in the friend group. He did this, no doubt, as a genuine friend voicing honest concern.

Soon he found the group as a whole was engaging with him less often. He received fewer invitations and clear signs of separation. Before long, he was shut out and found himself back where he started: on the outside looking in.

Three conclusions can be drawn from these stories:

1. Hospitable friendliness is a social expectation and cultural norm in the South.

2. Being culturally prescribed, the friendliness that newcomers experience doesn't necessarily indicate desire for a more fully developed relationship.

3. The warmth of being included in a friendly social circle is contrasted by the cold animosity of being outside of it.

A close friend of the Detroit transplant from the previous story, a Southerner, describes how the culturally prescribed norm of friendliness affects our perceptions of others:

> If you asked "Who is the nicer person?" between the two of us, most people who know us would probably say me. I don't directly rock the boat like she does or call people out on their shortcomings—even though she's usually making a fair point or trying to help someone out. I also might not tell you if you had food stuck on your face because I wouldn't want you to be embarrassed. It's kind of like that. The spinach stuck in your teeth would embarrass you if you knew it was there, so rather than tell you so you can fix it, I just behave as if it doesn't exist. (I know this is probably wrong.) *She* would tell you there's spinach in your teeth. So who's being more friendly?
>
> In reality, she's probably a much better person than I am—not that I'm a typical Southerner and she's a typical Northerner. I don't think I'm a bad person, but I've seen her give a lot of herself for other people. She'll go way farther than I would ever go to help others. But still, our friends would probably say I was a "nicer" person.

Perceptions matter, of course. To be perceived as behaving in the appropriate way wins social approval and rewards in every culture. The "best" way is largely determined by cultural mores and expectations. So, if you understand the cultural lens through which you're being perceived, you can manage those perceptions and make yourself better understood. At the same time, by understanding the cultural pressures that drive the behavior of others, you can better understand their point of view.

Being friendly has its perks in the South. You can be friendly and "on good terms" with someone yet have no expectations of a more developed relationship. This can frustrate newcomers who read this out-of-the-gate friendliness as the beginning of some deeper possibilities (or, conversely, an invasion of privacy). But Southerners tend to feel that maintaining a mutually beneficial relationship doesn't necessarily require extraordinary closeness or intimacy. One can have close-knit friendship groups while maintaining larger and larger circles of less significant social connections.

In the rural South, where one's social connections may be limited by geographical circumstance, friendship groups or relational circles may include only a few close neighbors and relatives, thus magnifying their importance. But as this region becomes more populated and urbanized, the cultural propensity to build and maintain relationships can lead to a proliferation of social connections. Like overlapping patterns of concentric circles, these social connections are complex and can be difficult for outsiders to understand. For the Southern archetype studied here, these overlapping relational structures are the primary material from which society is built and ordered.

To illustrate this, let's consider another hypothetical story.

A Connecticut native joins his college roommate for Christmas break in Georgia. Having never been to the Deep South, Hayden takes the opportunity to do so with his trusted and respected friend John. They arrive a couple of days early and spend the time seeing John's small hometown. On Christmas Eve, John's mother sends them out for some last minute provisions. The first stop is the hardware store for some replacement strands of Christmas lights. Charlie has worked at the hardware store for as long as John can remember and, unsurprisingly, he's there when John and Hayden walk in. They give each other hearty hellos and catch up a bit before Charlie asks about John's family.

"How's your mama and them?"

"Oh, they're all doing fine. Mom's getting everything ready for tomorrow and doing her best to fatten us up. She's got us out running errands, but I'm guessing she just wanted us out of her way. We've been in for a couple of days already."

"Well, tell everybody I said hello and hope to see 'em soon."

"I will do, Charlie. How are Jane and Mike?" These were Charlie's children, one a few years older and the other a year younger than John. "Is he still at State?"

"He is, and by the looks of things he may be there forever. We're putting all our hope in Jane at this point," Charlie says with a wry smile.

"That's where I'd put my money," John replies, sending them both into open laughter.

"Good to see you, Rocket, and nice to meet you, son," he says to Hayden, shaking both their hands again. "Y'all have a nice break and a Merry Christmas."

"Thanks, Charlie. You too!"

After leaving the store, Hayden asks how John knows Charlie.

"He's Charlie. He's always been there."

"Why did he call you Rocket?"

"I used to build model rockets and was in the store a lot for parts and fuel. He called me Rocket from then on."

The young men continue on to the grocery. Walking through the parking lot, they hear a voice call their way: "Hey, Johnny Bee!" John looks up to see a former classmate who had known him long enough to remember this nickname originated on a third grade field trip when he sat on a nest of yellow jackets.

"Hey, Susan! How's it going?"

"Great! Everybody's in town, so Mom is very pleased for once. This is my third trip here today—she's keeping us busy."

"How's everybody doing?"

"They're all good," she says, going on to tell John about her family. "How's everybody over your way? How's your Mom?" John reports that she's doing well and introduces Hayden.

"Alright, tell everyone hello and Merry Christmas," she says.

"You too. Bye!"

They walk into the store and Hayden asks, "Johnny Bee?" John tells him the story as they walk toward the dairy section. But before they reach it, John recognizes another familiar face coming their way.

"Hello, Mr. Robertson," John says brightly.

"Hey, Stormy!" They shake hands and John introduces Hayden. Mr. Robertson asks about John and vice versa. "How's your Mama and them doing?" John declares everyone to be fine before asking about Mr. Robertson's people. They say goodbye and the young men finish off their shopping list.

On the way back home, John anticipates Hayden's question and explains where the nickname Stormy came from. "Mr. Robertson's son and I were friends when we were little kids. When I was about six, I showed up at their house after a storm in my swimming trunks and asked if he could come play in the mud puddles with me. He did, and for a couple of summers we would tromp around the neighborhood, playing in the mud and rain. He's called me Stormy since then. He goes to church with my Mom."

"Yeah, about that, why was everyone asking about your 'Mama'? Has she been sick or something?"

John laughs. "No. They're just being nice."

"Nice? Huh. It's weird. If he goes to church with your Mom, wouldn't he have just seen her?"

"I'm sure. Those two never miss a Sunday."

"Is it a big church?"

"Not even close."

"Well, wouldn't he know how she's doing if he just saw her—what, three days ago?" Hayden rubs his increasingly contorted brow in hope of solving this riddle. "Why would he need to ask you? Why did everybody ask you how she's doing?"

"Like I said, they're just being nice. Polite. Asking about my family. They're just friendly people."

Most Southerners no longer spend part of every conversation asking about your "mama" or "your people," but the same underlying message is still often expressed and understood by the archetypical Southerner. What is implied is a level of concern that demonstrates interconnectedness between the speakers. What is not said is that "I care about you and yours and will be here if you need to call on me." If Southern society is built on relational structures, these expressions of mutual concern and interest are rivets that serve to hold it together.

Rocket, Stormy, and Johnny Bee were all nicknames that connected John to his past. He had lived with them his whole life and they'd become his names, but again they carried other implications. Each speaker who used these alternate names for John was indicating and highlighting their mutual history together. Where Hayden heard a multitude of odd nicknames that seemed arbitrarily (and therefore insubstantially) applied, John only heard his name. But what John felt was the larger connection to his hometown and the people who live there. He believed they could be depended upon if the need arose, just as he would be there for them if required. No heavy lifting was necessary to maintain this level of interconnection. Simply acknowledging their shared past was enough.

John explained to Hayden that his hometown neighbors were just being polite and friendly, and this is how many Southerners would describe the conversational reflex of asking about someone's people. It *is* friendliness to the Southern mind. As such, it is culturally prescribed and can be faked for the sake of form. But it can also carry a significant cultural message: *we are interconnected and responsible to each other.*

Is the American South Distinctive?

Friendliness and hospitality are qualities often associated with the South, and Southerners are equally known for their love of tradition and an almost mystical sense of place. But friendliness and hospitality can be found across this generous nation, as can reverence for place and tradition. So can we really say that the South is distinctive in these regards? Perhaps the difference is in the *expression* of these qualities, and not the qualities themselves.

Let's back up further and ask the general question: In what ways is Southern culture distinct from the rest of the country? To answer this, we'll compare a composite of the "American character" with that of a Southerner. Then, we'll take a brief look at some literary heavyweights whose work captured the spirit and perspectives of their regional cultures, and we'll finish up with an outline of the dominant cultures carried into colonial America by our early fore-bears. In these three areas, we search for what marks the South as a distinctive American culture with its own com-munication style. This is not an exhaustive examination of these subjects but is meant, rather, to identify and explore unique characteristics of Southern culture.

Southern historian C. Vann Woodward identified four areas in which life down south fundamentally diverged from the larger American experience. Woodward was per-haps the most important historian to write about Southern culture in the crucial and highly charged period after World War II. His influence in the Civil Rights era reached far beyond the halls of academia and deep into the pub-lic dialogue.[1] Writing in 1958, he saw an America surging with economic expansion and filled with patriotic fervor, revealing the legendary American character. This American archetype was marked by abundance, success, a sense of moral innocence, and an abstract outlook that transcended place and custom.[2]

This wasn't true, however, for Southerners. Their Ameri-can experience was very different and offered little basis on which to construct a duplicate of the "American character." The first three of these qualities—abundance, success, and innocence—were denied because of the historical develop-ment of slavery and the war that ended it. But Woodward's fourth distinction indicated something more internal to each culture: abstract versus traditional perspectives on life.

ABUNDANCE

Where Americans could be described as a *People of Plenty*,* the Southern experience had long been a story defined by poverty. Woodward called this a "continuous and conspicuous feature of Southern experience since the early years of the Civil War." The Southern economy had vastly improved by the time of Woodward's writing and has grown dramatically since. But long historical experience—whether in poverty or abundance—leaves its mark on a culture. "That they should have been for so long a time a 'People of Poverty' in a land of plenty," Woodward wrote, "is one mark of enduring cultural distinctiveness."[4]

SUCCESS

The American character "is bottomed upon the profound conviction that nothing in the world is beyond its power to accomplish." This was according to historian Arthur M. Schlesinger, writing during World War II. The U.S. came out of the war buoyed by victory and an ever-expanding economy. There was good reason for Americans to feel confident and walk with a sure step. Woodward identified in the legend of the American character a feeling of invincibility and inevitable triumph.[5] The Vietnam War, Watergate, the War on Drugs, and the challenges of the "War on Terror" were yet to come, but even today, the sense of America as a success story and of Americans as a

---

* This is the title of a 1956 book by Southern historian David M. Potter who, according to Woodward, "persuasively advances the thesis that the most distinguishing traits of national character have been fundamentally shaped by the abundance of the American living standard."[3]

self-confident, can-do people runs strong. It remains a defining characteristic.

"This is but one of several American legends in which the South can participate only vicariously or in part," Woodward wrote. "For Southern history, unlike American, includes large components of frustration, failure, and defeat. It includes not only an overwhelming military defeat but long decades of defeat in the provinces of economic, social, and political life."[6]

It's been a century and a half since Appomattox. Most of those years saw rife poverty in the American South. Though the economy and opportunities for all Southerners have dramatically improved, these conditions, again, leave their mark. For generations, Southerners had no illusions of omnipotence or assured success.

MORAL INNOCENCE

A "legend of American innocence" sprang from the young country's success and abundance. Its opposite was found in Europe's Old World evils of feudalism, tyranny, monarchy, and aristocratic privilege. Americans felt they were a "regeneration of sinful man" born free and innocent of the European stain. This self-image allowed them a sense of moral pre-eminence as the chosen people of a New World.[7]

As for Southerners, Woodward asked, "How much room was there in the tortured conscience of the South for this national self-image of innocence and moral complacency?":

> Southerners have repeated the American rhetoric of self-admiration and sung the perfection of

American institutions ever since the Declaration of Independence. But for half that time they lived intimately with a great social evil and the other half with its aftermath. It was an evil that was even condemned and abandoned by the Old World, to which America's moral superiority was supposedly an article of faith.[8]

The South was preoccupied "with guilt, not innocence, with the reality of evil, not with the dream of perfection. Its experience in this respect … was on the whole a thoroughly un-American one."[9]

ABSTRACT OUTLOOK

"Americans are abstract," said writer Thornton Wilder (author of *Our Town* and *The Bridge of San Luis Rey*). "They are disconnected. They have a relation, but it is to everywhere, to everybody, and to always."[10]

Americans can find in environment no confirmation of their identity. . . . There is only one way in which an American can feel himself to be in relation to other Americans—when he is united with them in a project, caught up in an idea and propelled with them toward the future. There is no limit to the degree with which an American is imbued with the doctrine of progress. Place and environment are but décor to his journey. He lives not on the treasure that lies about him but on the promises of the imagination. "I am

I," he says, "because my plans characterize me."
Abstract! Abstract![11]

Wilder didn't include Southerners in his theory of American abstraction, though he did account for them by referring to Southern states as relics of an Old World system. "They were cut off, or resolutely cut themselves off, from the advancing tide of the country's modes of conscious-ness," he lectured in 1950. "Place, environment, relations, repetitions are the breath of their being."[12] Wilder saw this as evidence of a non-advancing culture, but many of his Southern contemporaries would likely have translated this as "home, family, tradition, duty" and declared them unas-sailable values worthy of aspiration.

This contrast of cultural perspectives—abstract versus traditional—may be at the center of our cross-cultural miscommunications.

In an earlier work,[13] Woodward saw clear examples of this contrast in literature. To him, the characters that populate the works of early twentieth-century Midwest-ern novelists "appear on the scene from nowhere, trailing no clouds of history, dissociated from the past."[14] He pro-claimed that Hemingway's characters appear even more flat in terms of historical perspective: "A Hemingway hero with a grandfather is inconceivable, and he is apparently quite as bereft of uncles, aunts, cousins, and in-laws, not to mention neighbors and poor relations."[15] As for New England au-thors, they "regularly pictured the individual starkly alone with his problems, his wilderness, or his God." Melville's characters "appear to live entirely in the present or the fu-ture and to concern themselves seldom with the past."

But of the Southern novelists, the historian found strong appeal in "their way of treating man not as an individual alone with his conscience or his God ... or alone at sea with a whale or a marlin, or alone in a ring with a bull, but as an *inextricable part of a living history and community*, attached and determined in a thousand ways by other wills and destinies of people he has only heard about"[16] (italics added).

Contrast this with how a protagonist of the Southern novelist Thomas Wolfe describes early twentieth-century, working class New Yorkers: "They lived like creatures born full grown into present time, shedding the whole accumulation of the past with every breath, and all their lives were written in the passing of each actual moment."[17]

Mississippian William Faulkner and Ralph Waldo Emerson from Massachusetts epitomize their respective regions like few American writers ever have. In their works, one finds the essence of their cultures' prescriptions for the "best" way to orient oneself in the world.

In Faulkner's great novel *Absalom, Absalom!*, central character Thomas Sutpen is made to lose everything—all his dreams and all he held dear. Faulkner once explained in an interview why Sutpen was rejected by society and eventually destroyed:

> He was not depraved—he was amoral, he was ruthless, completely self-centered. To me he is to be pitied, as anyone who ... does not believe that he belongs as a member of a human family, of *the* human family, is to be pitied. Sutpen didn't believe that. He was Sutpen. He was going to take

what he wanted because he was big enough and strong enough, and I think that people like that are destroyed sooner or later, because one has got to belong to the human family, and to take a responsible part in the human family. . . . [18]

Throughout Faulkner's work, we find a theme of the interconnectedness of all things through time. With Emerson, quite the opposite is true:

I hope in these days we have heard the last of conformity and consistency. Let the words be gazetted and ridiculous henceforward. . . . Let us affront and reprimand the smooth mediocrity and squalid contentment of the times, and hurl in the face of custom, and trade, and office, the fact which is the upshot of all history, that there is a great responsible Thinker and Actor working wherever a man works; that a true man belongs to no other time or place, but is the centre of things. Where he is, there is nature. [19]

In Faulkner's view, Sutpen was bound for destruction because he was self-centered and rejected his place in the "family" of mankind. Emerson implores his audience to see individual man as the center of all things, who should reject custom and his fellow man for their sins of conformity and consistency.

For Emerson, the best approach to the world begins with "I am." For Faulkner, it is unmistakably "We are." The same can be said of their respective cultures. In the South, the culturally endorsed concept of self begins with group identification, as in "*We are* of a proud tradition." For Yankees, the concept of self is more likely found with the abstract qualities of the individual, as in "*I am* who I choose to be."

This difference in self-orientation is not without cultural consequences or cultural antecedents. If we follow the histories of these regions further back, we quickly find ourselves in Merry Old England. But once there, we discover very different "mother" cultures that fundamentally opposed each other. These cultures were direct predecessors of the American North and South.

MOTHER CULTURES INTO MODERN PERSPECTIVES

The Puritans of Massachusetts and the Cavaliers of Virginia played dominant roles in the development of their regional cultures. Each group was driven to the New World to escape persecution by the other: the Puritan Parliamentarians in 1630 as the monarchy flexed its power, and the Royalist Cavaliers who fled Parliamentarian rule after 1642.

The English Civil War pitted these two groups and their contrasting ideas about society firmly against each other. John Winthrop led the first Puritans toward his "city on a hill" in the Massachusetts Bay where they endeavored as a chosen people of God to build a new kind of society. William Berkeley came to the Chesapeake Bay in Virginia to found another kind of ideal society—one that looked back to the aristocratic, hierarchical Cavalier system as its model of perfection.

The histories of these immigrant groups suggest an underlying clash of cultures. Perhaps this clash was antithetical enough to fuel three civil wars: the English Civil War, the American Revolution and the American Civil War, as author Kevin Phillips argues in *The Cousins' Wars*. And perhaps the underlying discord remains a source of conflict and misunderstanding.

There are many ways to contrast these seventeenth-century cultures. Obviously their politics—Royalist versus Parliamentarian—positioned them as oppositional forces at a critical moment in the development of English and American democracies. But what sort of cultural traits might have led to the contrasting "I am" versus "We are" perspectives evidenced in the works of Emerson and Faulkner?

The Puritans who flooded into New England from 1630 to 1641 were a product of their mother culture in East Anglia, the easternmost counties of England.[20] This was the most densely settled and commercially active region in England, with strong ties to the prosperous Dutch across the North Sea. Puritans on both sides of the Atlantic pursued democratic governments and capitalistic economies.[21] Once in the New World, they developed a society intended to be superior to its Old World predecessor in every way. The Puritan model would eventually spread throughout colonial New England, exerting a cultural domination based on its bustling commercial system and emphatic democratic spirit. "In Massachusetts, but also elsewhere in New

England, the stamp of East Anglia, its people and ideas, was writ large," Phillips writes.[22]

The Royalist Cavaliers who settled Virginia, on the other hand, were culturally linked to southern, and particularly southwestern, England.* It was here that large manorial estates replete with servants, tenant farmers, and lords of ancient lineages could be found in a semi-feudal society across the rural landscape. Huge tracts of wooded forests and large agricultural estates made for few town centers in the southwest.[24] Manors were the centers of life here, and they had been for a long time, as David Hackett Fischer points out in his excellent history, *Albion's Seed: Four British Folkways in America*. Estate boundaries and administrative divisions (indeed the hedgerows) "had already been in existence for many centuries before the Norman conquest." Kings Alfred and Athelred would recognize this area on the map as their very own Wessex.[25] Berkeley imported this Old World culture and administered its implementation over a thirty-five year period, firmly establishing a feudal Cavalier system in the Virginia tidewater of the American South.

SETTLEMENT PATTERNS

New England's settlement pattern reflected those of seventeenth-century East Anglia. In early Massachusetts, the now-familiar New England system of centralized villages, surrounding hamlets, and outlying farmsteads would spread throughout the region. Transplanted from East

---

* Though Jamestown had been founded in 1607, it was a "sickly settlement of barely 8,000 souls" when Berkeley arrived in 1642, according to historian Fischer.[23]

Anglia, this model has done well enough in New England to persist for over three centuries.[26]

The Cavaliers spread out across the Chesapeake Bay on large estates,[27] echoing the manorial system developed in southwest England. There were no great towns or urban areas. The Chesapeake economy relied on agriculture, and Cavalier lords spread their plantations far and wide to maximize the potential of their land and efforts.[28] The plantation was both the center of social life and economic activity. As time went by, dispersed rural neighborhoods of ten or twenty homes were common across a decentralized Virginia. Fischer sets the scene:

> As one generation succeeded another, neighborhoods tended to become kin-groups. Ties of blood and marriage created a web of increasing density. The members of these kin-neighborhoods worked together, played together, and went to church and court days together. They borrowed from one another, becoming also a network of credit and barter relationships.[29]

ECONOMIES

As the Massachusetts Bay Colony developed and offered up the agricultural commodities of a rich, unspoiled land, the Puritans began exporting their commercial goods. By 1645, the Connecticut Valley was sending thousands of bushels of grain to markets. Even as early as 1638, the shipping and trading business was highly active with more than a hundred vessels engaged in foreign export. This reflected an East Anglian tradition of commercial shipping in the North Sea.[30]

Puritan leaders recruited immigrants with some financial means and status, largely drawing newcomers from the skilled middle class. As a result, between fifty and sixty percent of immigrants had some skilled craft or trade. There were comparatively few slaves, though slavery was legal and practiced. Less than twenty-five percent of the overall population were servants, and most of these arrived as members of a household.[31] Once here, this predominantly middle-class population was strengthened by Puritan religious beliefs that resulted in a more equitable division of land.[32] This, combined with the furious Puritan work ethic, fueled a diverse economy and propelled growth.

Puritans are remembered for their intensely focused religious piety, but they were equally focused on developing their economies.[33] An egalitarian capitalism was taking its first steps in the New World. However, egalitarian ideals or religious principles would not keep New Englanders from vigorously entering the slave trade. Commerce was commerce: "Although New Englanders took their religion seriously, they did not permit it to interfere with their appreciation of the profits of slavery and the slave trade," writes John Hope Franklin in the great history of African Americans, *From Slavery to Freedom*.[34]

Meanwhile, Virginia's economic system developed around the plantation manor. Much like in southwest England, the primary economic activity was the production of staple agricultural commodities on large estates that were held by a minority of the population. The plantation was the center of social as well as economic life, and at the top of both were the gentlemen-farmers of Cavalier Virginia. Like the gentry in southwest England, the Cavaliers scorned work and valued idleness as an entitlement of their class. Contemptuous of trade and traders, they valued wealth for the luxuries and status it afforded them, not for its power to drive capitalistic economies.[35] The proprietary estate didn't exist for profit—it existed to maintain a family's station in society.[36] This way of life required a large underclass of servants and eventually slaves. "The culture of the English countryside," Fischer tells us, "could not be reproduced in the New World without this rural proletariat."[37]

While Lord Berkeley was recruiting Cavaliers to be Virginia gentlemen, he also ran an open labor draft for indentured servants. This was intended to satisfy the tremendous demand for agricultural laborers on the large plantations. Seventy-five percent of seventeenth-century immigrants to Virginia landed as indentured servants.[38] When the practice proved problematic, the aggressive implementation of race-based slavery became the answer for Cavalier lords. In both Virginia and southwest England, an elite class of about ten percent of the population ruled over large numbers of poor and a minority of "middling" groups. In Virginia, only about thirty percent were artisans. Two-thirds were unskilled laborers who worked mostly as tenant farmers.[39] This economy was solely focused around the plantation.

In the end, the Cavalier lifestyle would gobble up whatever productive gains were brought from the land. Chronic indebtedness was the result of Cavalier economics, just as it had been in southwest England.[40] From the beginning, wealth in Virginia was concentrated in the hands of a very few at the top. There it foundered inside a feudal fantasy.

CIVIC CULTURE

Perhaps East Anglia's most important endowment to New England was political and governmental: a "civic culture of high literacy, town meetings, and a tradition of freedom reaching back to Saxon days," as Phillips puts it.[41] East Anglia was anti-Royalist and pro-Parliament, with local democratic systems that developed over centuries before their immigration across the Atlantic.[42] "This was a heritage of liberty New Englanders were proud to share—and would refer to many times in 1774–1775."[43]

New England's founders would apply their system of democracy in the New World and carry it further than their East Anglian cousins. But, the Puritans present a bit of a paradox: they sought and found freedom in the New World, yet institutionalized the invasion of personal liberties in the name of God. For example, the early Puritans emphasized the nuclear family as an "instrument of their highest religious purposes," Fischer writes, and to this end, town selectmen were sometimes required to inspect households and insure "good order" of the family who lived there.[44] This "ordered liberty" seems a strange version of freedom. However, the ultimate Puritan goal was religious utopia, and they meant to use an integrated church-state authority to reach that goal. The key feature of "ordered liberty" was that society's laws (no matter how invasive or cruel) were, more or less, equally applied. The Old World system of inherited rank and privilege was firmly rejected.

No one was above God's law, though slaves were denied its mercies.

The Virginia Cavaliers, in contrast, inherited a subjective approach to governance: the law was applied according to who you were. The key feature of the Cavalier political structure was its hierarchical class and rank system. At the top was the King of England. More locally, it was the gentry as plantation lords. This hierarchy and its unquestionable authority (based on "ancient and noble" lineages) would ensure the law worked in their favor. "The government was an instrument—a club in their hands, which they never used on themselves," writes historian Morris Talpalar in *The Sociology of Colonial Virginia*.[45]

From 1660 to the American Revolution, the Virginia Council would be dominated by just five related family connections. Every member of the Council until 1775 would be descended from one who served in 1660. The carefully planned marriages of cousins were designed to "create a web of kinship as dense as that of the Roman patriciate" that did indeed rule over all Virginia, Fischer explains.[46] This went for all Virginia civic institutions: the Royal Council, the Houses of Burgesses and Commons, the offices of Sherriff—they would all be controlled by a powerful, interconnected oligarchy that saw itself as an elite class. There could be no equal treatment under their law because they had no equals. The outcome was a system of governance that applied the rules subjectively based on the particulars of *who* was being governed.

CULTURAL OUTLOOK

The Puritan settlements of New England were not exact duplicates of each other. There were variations in religious beliefs, civic laws, economic activities, and so on. But nearly all New Englanders agreed on one thing: the Old World Royalist system was spiritually, morally, and economically corrupt. They looked forward to a New World power structure, one they were making with their very own hands.

The Virginia Cavaliers displayed a profound cultural conservatism that sought to re-create the lord-and-manor system of southwest England. The elite believed their inherited privilege was unquestionable. Just as they looked backward to prove their rank in society, they looked back to the plantation system of southwest England to build their economy. Isolated by their settlement pattern and inward-focused economy, early Virginians had little left to celebrate but their noble tradition. The Cavaliers were distrustful of foreigners and foreign ideas—traditional prejudices of English gentlemen—and their outlook for the future mirrored its past. This society would be an aristocracy, and it would vigorously defend the traditional social order against any threat.[47]

These brief histories don't tell us the full story of the Puritans and the Cavaliers, but they do provide insight into the I- and We-oriented cultures that developed out of them. To be sure, contradictory interpretations can be made of both groups. One could argue that the Puritans displayed group-oriented behavior through the village settlement pattern, the central role of church congregations, or their cooperation in commerce. Likewise, the Cavalier quest for an aristocratic lifestyle was plainly self-indulgent and could therefore be interpreted as an individualistic culture. However, the complexity of human behavior requires us to look deeper into the American psyche if we hope to find the source of the Southern distinction. In these pages, we take a broad approach and will accept the presence of complexity and gray areas.

The contrasting perspectives of an I- versus a We-orientation produce different cultural imperatives, which lead to starkly dissimilar ways of communicating as well. The quintessential New Englander, Emerson, and the quintessential Southerner, Faulkner, would have recognized these imperatives in their respective seventeenth-century forebears.

An individual-oriented, I-perspective culture revealed itself in colonial New England:

- A highly commercial economy, urban settlement pattern, and a more tolerant attitude (eventually) exposed New Englanders to a multiplicity of ideas and customs. There was no ancient system guiding the hands of Puritans—they were remaking the world based on their own new ideas.

- The Old World model of class and rank aristocracies was rejected, and land was spread more equitably. New Englanders were fostering a meritocratic system that rewarded individual achievement.

- The New England civic structure was more egalitarian, and its leaders aspired to an equal application of the law. Their sense of legal fairness ideally held individuals to account for their actions and punished accordingly, regardless of their group associations.

Evidence of a group-oriented, We-perspective culture can be found throughout Cavalier Virginia:

- A dispersed settlement pattern, an archaic economy, and an emphatic cultural bigotry meant Virginians *were isolated* with and *dependent upon* their group.
- Class and rank were fixed, and social mobility was virtually non-existent. The group to which you were born defined both who you were and who you would remain.
- A hierarchical power structure fostered a subjective application of laws, making impossible a universal and equal system of justice. This particularist mindset (which showed favor or not based on *who* needed it and *who* could give it) extended throughout the aristocratic class and reached into lower-class kin groups and neighborhood alliances. Your group association would determine your treatment under the law, not necessarily your individual actions.

To be sure, much has changed in the nearly four centuries since the Puritans and Cavaliers crossed the Atlantic, but some things remain. Chief among them are the contrasting I- and We-perspectives, which produce different cultural norms for each group. This divergence continues to define important psychological and behavioral contrasts between Northerners and Southerners.

Of course, Southern culture was not shaped by the Cavaliers alone. (Nor was New England influenced solely by the Puritan groups.) There have been many cultural influences in the American South: the French and Creole in Louisiana, the Spanish in south Florida, the Scottish Highlanders at Cape Fear, the Gullah of Lowland South Carolina, the Asian influence along the lower Mississippi, the Germans in Appalachia and East Texas, and so on.

This constant movement and resettling of peoples produces complex local histories that are resistant to generalizations. But the Cavaliers—along with the African American and Scotch-Irish cultures—played dominant roles in the developing South. We've already seen how the Cavalier culture fostered a We-oriented people. Next, we turn briefly to the other two mother cultures in search of a We- or I-orientation.

CLAN CULTURES OF WEST AFRICA AND NORTH BRITAIN

African Americans were *forced* into the Cavalier culture. Whether their freedom was stolen in Africa or whether born without it, African Americans in the slave-holding South had to adopt the Cavalier way in order to survive it. The class and rank aristocracy was doubly firm in holding the slave in place, and the color of his skin would always identify the group to which he belonged.

The West African cultures from which these slaves were taken are largely considered to have been We-oriented cultures. For the most part, these cultures were organized around the clan or tribal social system. (These terms are interchangeable.) West Africa had seen—and still maintained—city-state kingdoms, urban commercial centers, and a variety of economies. But the stable social organization of the clan system formed the foundational political unit when European slavers began arriving on their coasts.[48]

In some ways, clan systems epitomize a We-oriented perspective. "We," in the tribal sense, is the source of culture, livelihood, and personal identity. The interdependency of clan members—their reliance on each other—would motivate them to account for the group, not just themselves. Tradition and place figured highly in group cohesiveness and prosperity. "The immediate family, the clan [the larger family], and the ethnic community undergirded every aspect of [West African] life," Franklin writes.[49]

African American slaves had the Cavalier way of life thrust upon them, but their own African cultural heritage would greatly impact the larger, New World culture emerging in the South. Slave populations forged a new, African *and* American culture from their various cultural backgrounds. Adapting to the terrible fate of enslavement in a hostile land, they depended on this developing new culture for survival and to one day free them from that fate. Both We-oriented cultures—African American and white Cavalier—would be hugely impacted by their interaction with the other, eventually intertwining around one way of life.

A third dominant mother culture to the American South came from the borderlands in northern Britain and is often referred to as "Scotch-Irish." These eighteenth-century immigrants brought with them a clan-based social system shaped by seven hundred years of borderland warfare between England and Scotland. Until these two kingdoms were united (and well after, too), the north of England and the Scottish lowlands were a lawless borderland organized into its many warring clans. Over the centuries, population movements between this region and Ireland across the Irish Sea were numerous, culminating in the Scottish colonization of Ulster and the later English-led conquest of all of Ireland.

When the English and Scottish thrones were combined, the pacification process meant the rules were slowly changing in the borderlands. The clan system had fostered a warrior culture that had been beneficial to the goals of the warring kingdoms. No longer at war, the aristocracy began to reassert their property rights in the region and to push the old warring clans out of the picture. The changing political and economic conditions combined to create an eighteenth-century fervor among the borderlanders to leave for the New World. The term "Scotch-Irish," as it is used here, refers to these Scottish, Irish, and northern English immigrants who poured into the Appalachian highlands from Pennsylvania to Georgia before pushing further west toward the Mississippi River.[50]

The clan-organized social structure of the borderland Scotch-Irish translated well in the dangerous backcountry of the New World. Still the homeland of highly organized Native American nations, the backcountry would become a lawless, disputed territory marked by violent wars between the populations. The clan structure made group survival possible in very difficult conditions. As Fischer explains, "The borderers were more at home than others in this anarchic environment, which was well suited to their family system, their warrior ethic, their farming and herding economy, their attitudes toward land and wealth, and their ideas of work and power."[51]

Survival for the North Britons and their New World Scotch-Irish descendants was dependent upon the success of their clan. Interdependent in every way, early backcountry Americans would continue to see the world with a We-perspective. The group (or clan) was not only the source of survival and culture—it was the source of personal identity. This We-orientation of the Scotch-Irish would remain strong in the backcountry, intertwining another dominant cultural strand into the story of the American South.

THE DUTCH IN MANHATTAN, AND THE CARIBBEAN IN CAROLINA

Two final cultural influences must be considered and accounted for if we want to properly set these regional scenes. The first comes from the colonial Dutch who settled a noteworthy island at the mouth of the Hudson River. The second involves colonial Carolina and the enduring influence it would have on the development of the Deep South. Both carried with them the respective I- and We-orientations of the larger cultures developing in these regions. We'll spend a little more time in the Deep South, as its politics and economy would forever shape Southern culture and the country as a whole.

The dominance of Puritan culture in the American Northeast is evidenced by the triumph of a highly commercial democratic capitalism, an achievement fostered and fought for by determined hands. But it's impossible to think of a "Yankee culture" without accounting for the Dutch and the city they called New Amsterdam.

The two groups were Old World neighbors and had significant cultural interaction and overlap across the North Sea. East Anglia bore a "strong and unique Dutch imprint" in its "land reclamation, engineering, agriculture, art, and architecture," as Phillips writes. The East Anglians absorbed these influences and yet remained thoroughly English. This process would be repeated in the New World. "Like its principal parent region, New England easily assimilated its scattering of Dutch, French Huguenot, Fleming, and Walloon immigrants."[52]

The Dutch had been in the region longer than the Puritans, settling along the Hudson River and founding a place now known as New York City. The colony was run by the Dutch West India Company as a commercial enterprise, and its settlers were more occupied with extracting resources from a rich land for market than they were in establishing a permanent Dutch-American culture. Where the Puritans combined a robust, burgeoning commerce with their religious beliefs as a chosen people in a new holy land, the Dutch remained focused on commerce, showing no interest in founding a New World utopia.[53]

On the eve of the American Revolution, the distinctive and cohesive Puritan culture—over 80% white Protestants of English ancestry—numbered more than a million strong and had founded colonies in Connecticut, New Hampshire, southern Maine, eastern Vermont, northern Ohio, upstate New York, Long Island, and eastern New Jersey. By this time they were known as "Yankees."[54]

The Dutch in America didn't expand far beyond the settlement's original boundaries, and by 1790, less than 100,000 people of Dutch descent lived in all of the newly founded United States.[55] This doesn't diminish the impact of the Dutch on New York and, through that city's influence, the rest of the United States. Perhaps their most lasting and important contribution to American culture was also what limited the potential impact of a *Dutch*-American culture: ethnic toleration and diversity. Rather than force Dutch customs and beliefs onto everyone in the colonial settlement—something the Puritans and Cavaliers vigorously engaged in—the Dutch allowed people from many other cultures to live in their territory and practice their own beliefs and customs. Having witnessed centuries of European wars, the highly-commercial Dutch had learned that tolerating other ethnicities was good for business and indeed enriched the fabric of their own culture.

"The Netherlands of this time was the melting pot of Europe," writes historian Russell Shorto in *The Island at the Center of the World*. Manhattan reflected "the same features of tolerance, openness, and free trade that existed in the home country."[56] But in New England, Dutch culture was subsumed under a tidal wave of English immigration. Given the importance of New York (and the Dutch impact on the East Anglian English), Dutch influence on American culture shouldn't be underestimated. However, in the end, it would be Yankee ideas and Yankee determination that charted the course of this great American city.

Both of these colonial cultures brought an I-orientation to the cultural mix. Meanwhile, along the Southern coast, a We-oriented culture was about to establish a most influential port city.

Charleston was founded in 1670 as the Carolina colony's port city. The rights to settle and rule the Lowcountry were granted to a group of eight Englishmen known as the Lords Proprietor. They supported Charles II in the English Civil War and helped reinstall him to the monarchy. The reward for these Royalist elite was the charter to Carolina. Though its founders had much in common with their peers in Tidewater Virginia, a distinctive strain of Cavalier-era culture developed in Lowcountry Carolina. It would become a model for the frontier lands to the west that we know as the Deep South.

Carolina resembled the colonies of the Caribbean more than Virginia, and this resemblance was carried across the Deep South as frontier land became U.S. territory. In Virginia, the elite landholders lived in the colony and tirelessly pursued its formation as an ideal Cavalier society. Quite the opposite was true in the Caribbean. Absentee landlords ruled from across the Atlantic, far away from the equatorial diseases and brutal conditions of their island plantations. These English landlords had no high ideals about forming cohesive societies in the New World. They were purely in it for the profit, which they received at home and in great abundance.[57] A glance at the Caribbean system shows how different it was from Virginia.

The sugar cane plantations that dominated the Caribbean after 1645 required a massive importation of slaves. For example, Barbados saw the number of slaves swell from only a few hundred in 1640 to 20,000 in just ten years.[58] By 1680, the island had as many as 40,000 slaves and only 23,000 free whites.[59] As white overseers became increasingly outnumbered by the enslaved population, fear of rebellion drove them to enact and enforce brutal slave codes.

This pattern—a high ratio of slaves to free people, harsh codes to quell rebellion, and the rapid ballooning of population to satisfy explosive demand for plantation crops—would be echoed in the Deep South. By 1790, in the three counties of Carolina's Lowcountry, there were less than 30,000 whites and as many as 80,000 slaves. Compare this to eastern Virginia where 300,000 whites controlled about half as many slaves.[60] The Southern back-country at this time had about 450,000 whites, including over 100,000 from Carolina's "Upcountry," and these settlements typically included less than ten percent slave populations (often much less). The differences were stark.[61]

Western expansion from Carolina began with Georgia's founding in 1733 as a non-slave state. This status would only hold until 1750, however, when settlers demanded the legalization of slavery and embraced a Lowcountry style of slave-based agriculture. To compare numbers, Georgia had 6,000 whites and 3,000 blacks living in its new boundaries in 1760. By 1773, the colony would have 18,000 whites and 15,000 blacks, almost all of them slaves. According to Franklin, "Much of Georgia's slave code ... was taken from the South Carolina code, and it reflected South Carolina's experience rather than Georgia's."[62]

Western exploration by frontiersmen into Alabama, Mississippi, and Louisiana paved the way for the expansion of plantation agriculture to the Mississippi River. Native American lands were wrested from them, and white settlers rushed to claim the prizes as their own. Wealthy landowners from the coasts saw tremendous opportunity to raise the super-commodity of the day on these super-fertile and recently-emptied lands.[63] Where sugar production was the center of life in the seventeenth-century Caribbean, it was rice and indigo in early Carolina. From the dawn of the nineteenth century, King Cotton was destined to remake the Deep South in its own image. This territory would populate quickly with just as many slaves as whites in a rush to feed the hungry textile mills in England, Massachusetts, and beyond. The industrial revolution was in full swing.

Louisiana, Mississippi, and Alabama became states in 1812, 1817, and 1819 respectively. Their populations would balloon until the Civil War. In 1810, the Mississippi/Alabama region held about 40,000 people. Only ten years later, the population had swelled to 200,000, and by 1840, nearly one million people lived in the region, roughly half of whom were slaves.[64] On the eve of the Civil War, these two states held 1.75 million people, 900,000 of whom lived in bondage.[65]

Slaves were often the majority in the Deep South, and slave codes were designed to be harsh enough to ensure submission. The relative newness of the area, combined with the quick population explosion needed to support a plantation economy, left a lasting mark on this part of the country. By 1960, Mississippi and Alabama had a combined population of five-and-a-half million, along with the most egregious racism and human rights abuses in the United States. Today, they combine to total eight million people who continue the long march toward equality for all races and ethnicities. While the states of the Deep South contributed much to the history and makeup of the South as a whole, the demise of slavery resulted in a collapsed economy and a bankrupted social system from which this part of the South would be the last to recover.

Though distinctive in many ways, the people of the Deep South also had much in common with the people of Cavalier Virginia and the Southern backcountry. In fact, many had come from these places to find their own fortunes and establish their own dynasties on the rich and ready Delta lands. They, too, would spread out on isolated plantations or farms, practice a staple-based mono-agriculture, and find few challenges to their cultural norms. But the Deep South developed much more quickly around this unsustainable economic system—one that would be destroyed in just a few short decades. The reverberations of its downfall can still be felt today, giving this region a distinctive set of qualities within the American South.

Beyond the political creation that was the Confederate States of America or the aftermath of its destruction, the most important shared quality of the people of the Deep South, the Upper South, and the Appalachian backcountry is their fundamental cultural outlook. They saw the world with a "We are" mindset, and they still do today.

Southern culture would be forged from the dominant Cavalier, African American and Scotch-Irish cultures, which were forever joined by a history that led to Confederate secession. The culture developed by the Puritans assimilated and absorbed other cultures, spreading across the Northeast, the Midwest, and even to the edge of the

Pacific Ocean. Eventually, its political and economic structures would come to dominate a continent.

Embedded in these mother cultures were the contrasting We- and I-orientations. These have profound implications on how people understand society and their place within it. They shape how individuals *conceive themselves*—a most fundamental psychological frame through which we see and interact with the world.

You'd be hard pressed to find many modern Southerners arguing against the principles of American democracy or American capitalism. (Hashing out details of how these should be maintained would be another matter.) But the interconnected, We-perspective Southerner has remained the cultural archetype. Not every Southerner is We-oriented, nor is every Northerner I-oriented. And even within the archetypes, there is variation in *how much* someone represents these characteristics.

The key to improving interpersonal communication between Southerners and non-Southerners—the point of this book—begins by recognizing the differences between these I- and We-orientations. They affect every aspect of our behavior.

CHAPTER THREE

The Highs and Lows in American Life

"We are" and "I am" are contrasting worldviews passed from one generation to the next by culture. Foundational to our psychology, these perspectives carry a host of characteristics related to behavior and communication. They are starting points from which everything else is ordered, making society look quite different through the prism of a "We" culture than through that of an "I" culture. They drive our psychological concerns, desires, needs, and preferences. Most importantly to our present endeavor, these worldviews shape how we interact and communicate with one another.

One way to understand the differences between these two types of cultures is through the High and Low Context model. This sociological tool examines how much a culture tends to depend on non-verbal (that is, contextual) information in communication. High Contexters depend on it a lot and Low Contexters much less so. The I-oriented culture of the Northeast displays qualities that mark it as a Low Context culture, and, in fact, the United States is widely regarded by social scientists as such.[1] However, the We-oriented culture of the South exhibits a different set of characteristics that place it firmly on the High Context side of the spectrum. An exploration of this High/Low Context model yields insight into the communication behavior of each type and opens the door to better cross-cultural interactions.

In the physical sciences, the attributes of matter or physiology can be categorized in terms of their measurable physical properties. But the social sciences pursue a less tangible subject: the qualities and properties of human behavior. There are many ways to define and describe human behavior. This is especially true within the academic fields studying its many complexities. The High/Low Context model is employed here for its usefulness to our mission and for the wide acceptance of its precepts in the social sciences.

High Context and *Low Context* refer to both a style of communication and the type of culture associated with that style.[2] Members of High Context cultures tend to depend on *contextual* information to carry a lot of meaning in conversations. People of Low Context cultures tend to rely less on context, recognizing instead the *content* of the message as the primary (if not sole) conveyer of meaning. The most influential and important form of context is that of the culture itself—its ways, beliefs, and customs. High Contexters see the influence of culture as strong and permeating in everyday life. Low Contexters see culture as less influential and instead seek an internal compass for guidance.[3]

The High/Low Context model was introduced by anthropologist Edward T. Hall in his 1976 book *Beyond Culture*. It should be understood as a spectrum, where the far ends represent the Highest and Lowest Context cultures, and along the middle are cultures that reflect gradients of these qualities. Hall proposes examples from art and law to illustrate the contrasting approaches of High and Low Context speech.[4]

In great paintings, the contextual elements of light, brushstroke, and color often relate more of the artist's message than the subject itself. Through contextual inference, we perceive elements of emotion or lack thereof, fluidity or permanence, boldness or timidity, and many other potential layers of meaning. Students of a specific artist can infer even more because they know the context of the artist's life and development. In this way, the specific meanings of an artist's work may be fully accessed only by those who speak that artist's contextual "language" of light, brushstroke, color, and other stylistic elements.

The Low Context speech of U.S. legal proceedings provides an opposing illustration. There, little is understood or recognized through inference. Every message is spelled out in excruciatingly explicit language. Like contracts and contract law, extremely Low Context communication carries only the meaning of what is clearly stated—unstated contextual information is not recognized as meaningful.

High and Low Context—as contrasting styles of speech—are associated with many other cultural characteristics. Chief among these are the contrasting We- or

I-orientations of self-identity. Listed below are three aspects of the psychological self that help explain some of the differences between High and Low Context cultures. These are generalizations that represent the far ends of the High/ Low spectrum. Most cultures would display only degrees of these qualities.

THE SOURCE OF SELF-IDENTITY

Members of High Context cultures draw their self-identities from the group or groups to which they belong.[5] Family, neighborhood, occupation, friend groups, and civic associations are all potential sources of the High Contexter's self-identity. The resulting "We are" perspective comes from the intertwining of individual and group identities.

For Low Contexters, the source of self isn't found in group associations, but within individuals themselves.[6] Low Contexters find it preposterous to suggest that self-identity is derived from external sources. For them, groups are collections of individuals. They may have much in common and share common goals, but each individual within the group remains just that—an internally conceived individual with an "I am" perspective of themselves and the world.

THE CONCEPT OF SELF IN SOCIETY

Because self-identity is intertwined with group identity, High Contexters are driven to secure the integrity and harmony of their groups. This is prioritized, but presents a dilemma as the individual moves from one set of group characteristics to another. In order to maintain group harmony and integrity across various group settings, the High Contexter must be a bit chameleon-like. As High

Contexters move through the variety of groups to which they belong, the self is understood as expressing its various qualities according to the context at hand.[7] Different contexts call for different behavior as individual consistency takes a back seat to group harmony. This means High Context behavior can be greatly impacted by the particulars of setting, present company, and the state of relationships between those present.

For Low Contexters, who perceive the self as internally constructed and driven, *consistency* of character in all settings is prioritized.[8] This is a higher cultural imperative than maintaining group harmony because self-identity is found within. The integrity of the individual—not the group—secures self-identity. Low Contexters moving through their various groups and personal associations are motivated to present themselves in a similar way regardless of their environment. Ideally, a complete and stable identity is established across all settings. As a result of this self-conception, context has a much *lower* impact on their behavior.

THE ROLE OF SELF IN SOCIETY

High Contexters are interconnected and feel obligated to support the groups to which they belong.[9] Since self-identity is largely defined by group membership, High Contexters feel duty-bound to serve group needs and defend group integrity. Many specific obligations and duties can be required and are determined by a specific group's nature. A son's duties to his father are different than a perceived obligation to throw a party for a friend. Or to help a neighbor move a couch. But they are all very real, and failing to fulfill an obligation can be seen as a slight against the relationship and the group as a whole. Fulfilling those duties cements group membership, which grants the security of mutual social assistance through belonging.

The Low Contexter views society as an organization of self-construed individuals. Their top priorities are autonomy, personal territory, and privacy.[10] Naturally, Low Contexters cooperate with and assist each other, but the sort of identity-challenging sense of obligation found in High Context systems isn't the cultural norm. Their I-oriented perspective leads them to expect that only explicit agreements obligate them to anyone else. Low Context cultures are more likely to institutionalize social assistance through their governments, and through these institutions, they provide members security and promote the primary goal of autonomy.

The psychological needs and pressures of High and Low Context cultures are fundamentally different, creating fundamental differences in social behavior. Satisfying these needs and pressures leads to cultural norms which establish the "right" way to behave and interact with others.

A High Contexter's We-orientation ties his or her identity to the group, elevating both the importance of maintaining group harmony and the influence of group culture on its members. These two characteristics mirror well-known qualities of Southern life: culturally prescribed friendliness (protecting group harmony) and strong traditions (resulting from the influence of group culture).

The I-orientation of Low Contexters drives them to maintain personal integrity, even if that risks the harmony of the group. Tradition is less influential to individuals whose source of identity is perceived to be internal, discovered only by their own experience. Low Contexters protect their unique identity by securing personal autonomy.

Context is an essential aspect of how the human mind efficiently processes information. We use it all the time to interpret and move through the world. The contexts of place, time, and activity pre-inform us (based on experience) of what to expect from any given situation. We walk into a bagel shop during the morning rush and expect to find a line. We attend our nephew's elementary school music recital and expect something less than the Vienna Philharmonic. We go to a ballpark and expect hot dogs.

In more fundamental ways, our subconscious minds are always working on pattern recognition, and our species is pretty good at it. We hear the muddled heckling of a baseball fan from across the stadium, but we understand the gist of their speech. We catch just a glimpse of a street scene and use context to fill in the blanks. We somehow spot the snake from among the many downed branches along a hiking trail. We are pattern seekers and context users by full rights from a long evolutionary process.[11]

Culture itself assists us in the pattern-seeking and information-sorting process. Its values, qualities, and norms seem natural to those within it. But not everyone (or every culture) grants the same role to cultural context in everyday life. Some use it more and some less.

High Context communication relies on a *high* level of contextual information to relate a speaker's full meaning. The context can be based on situation, present company, place, and many other circumstantial or psychological factors. Examples of High Context communication can be found inside specialized occupations where there's a lot of shared contextual knowledge. For example, a long-partnered carpenter and helper can work together and leave much unsaid because they share a contextual knowledge of their work. The helper knows what tool is needed next or what board is required based on the context of the situation, and he can communicate with the carpenter without saying what's obvious to them both. It's understood as shared knowledge. The same could be said of doctors, software engineers, or specialists within many other occupations.

Outside of the workplace, close friendships or relationships (like a marriage) can develop very High Context communication methods, relying heavily on shared contextual meanings. "Inside" jokes or "inside" knowledge are common in these High Context environments in which much more is communicated than what is explicitly spoken. The rest is seamlessly inferred by the listener from tone of voice, body language, silence, or any number of other non-verbal communications. These occupational and relational examples transcend cultural boundaries and illustrate how High Context communication occurs in many environments.

High Context communication as a culture-wide norm is also dependent on inside information—or specialized knowledge—being shared throughout the group. However, this shared, inside knowledge is all about the normative behavior and beliefs of the culture itself. Because We-oriented cultures emphasize the central role of the group, the context of shared cultural norms and beliefs becomes the backdrop upon which verbalized speech is placed.

Traditional Japanese culture is considered a very High Context system, one that uses a great deal of cultural context in communication. The formal Japanese Tea Ceremony demonstrates how the context of cultural tradition can impose itself into conversation. Context *is* the communication in the Tea Ceremony.

A glance at this 800-year old custom reveals a highly refined practice in which everything has its proper place. The host, guest of honor, and other guests are all assigned specific places that denote their roles. Utensils, placemats, flower arrangements, calligraphy, and landscaping are all carefully chosen and placed according to season and occasion of the ceremony. The host's every move is done with consideration of the peacefulness of the space and his guests. Participants seek a spiritual satisfaction obtained through silent contemplation in the tranquil setting. The host's goal is to create a placid arena for communication, but spoken conversation is generally limited to talk about the items of the ceremony itself—utensils, displayed art, flower arrangements, and the like. Little of the true meaning of the Tea Ceremony is actually verbalized, but it is highlighted everywhere in the context. The true meaning has to do with upholding traditional cultural goals of living in harmony, learning respect, seeking purity, and embracing tranquility. These conversations don't necessarily require verbalized speech.[12]

For very High Context cultures, most communication exists within the framework of an ever-present context of norms and beliefs, like the Tea Ceremony. A culture less High Context than Japan—like that of the American South—exhibits a lesser degree of contextual reliance. But don't be fooled. The context of culture is still abundantly present in the interpersonal communication of Southerners, as is their reliance on High Context speech. To be a successful High Context communicator in the South, one has to "read between the lines" of what is said to infer the full meaning of the speaker. As a hypothetical example, let's turn to the tea of America (coffee) and the ritualized arena of its delivery (the coffee shop).

Waylon leaves work early on a Friday and heads toward his favorite coffee shop. He's relaxed, feeling good about the world and generous of spirit towards it. There's a long weekend in front of him, and the crisp spring day stirs a primal joy in his heart. In short, everything is coming up Waylon.

His plan is to kick off the weekend with a late and leisurely lunch. Walking up to the entrance, he notices another patron round the corner a few paces behind him. He opens the door and steps back for her to pass through. She thanks him and offers him his place back in line, but he refuses. He's in no hurry this afternoon. They continue to chat about the weather and the neighborhood while waiting to place their orders.

"Hey," the barista says to Waylon with a tone of recognition. "How's it going?"

"Pretty freaking fantastic, John," Waylon responds with a playful smile. "The spring air is bringing out the best in me, I think. How's everything here?"

"Great. Very busy today, and we've got plans for the season opener later at the ballpark—so we're feeling pretty good about it too!"

Waylon congratulates him on his plans and places his order. He sets up camp in a sunbeam that lies across his favorite table in the place. After eating, he kicks back with a strong cup of coffee, pulls out some casual reading, and begins to ponder his gloriously open weekend.

It was already toward the end of lunch service when Waylon arrived, and soon he had lost track of time inside his cozy sunbeam. Barista John sweeps up as a colleague empties carafes of coffee. Waylon notices he is the last patron in the place and remembers the staff's baseball game. He scrambles to pack up his things, but before he finishes, John arrives to ask if he can help with anything else or if, maybe, he'd like to join them at the baseball game. Waylon thanks him but declines the kind offer.

"I was just about to take off. Y'all enjoy the game, and I'll see you soon. Great sandwich and coffee, as always—thanks so much!"

Context plays a significant role in this High Context environment and reveals itself in four ways:

The context of cultural tradition. Waylon's sense of his proper role in society drives him to behave in the neo-chivalrous manner of opening the door for someone else. Group traditions, elevated to the cultural level, become a vehicle for identifying with and supporting the group—an imperative in High Context systems because personal and group identities are intertwined. Holding the door open for a lady is something a gentleman should do, according to Waylon's cultural tradition, and he does it naturally without having to think about it much. For upholding tradition and for the good show of friendliness, he's rewarded with group acceptance and reciprocated friendliness.

The context of group dynamics. The We-orientation of High Contexters produces cultures that are more focused on group qualities than is the case among Low Contexters. In the mundane coffee shop interaction, we find a collection of people who are willing to view this public environment as holding some level of group status. Maintaining group harmony is a cultural reflex in the South, so the participants set about establishing it through small talk and reminders of previous connection. In High Context interactions, politeness and pleasantness are expected,[13] and this behavior shows support and respect for the dynamics of the group.

The subtext of small talk. Waylon and the others were quick to engage in small talk about the weather and the state of business at the shop. Small talk exists in most cultures and can even act as a way to maintain social distance. But Waylon's small talk is more personal and is based on an existing connection with John. Both are driven to bridge the divide of social distance rather than secure it. While small talk may not communicate much important information about the subjects discussed, what *is* important for High Contexters in these exchanges plays out in the subtext: *we are interconnected with each other.* Obviously, the coffee shop patrons don't represent Waylon's closest group identification, but still the cultural drive to solidify relational bonds is evident. Small talk accomplishes this with little effort, and satisfies the We-oriented sensibilities of High Contexters.

High Context speech. Barista John wants all of the guests out of the building so he and the rest of the staff can attend the baseball game. To send this message to potential malingerers like Waylon, John employs an indirect method of communication. First, he tells them about the staff's plan for the game. Later, while sweeping up, he asks Waylon if there's anything else he can get for him, indirectly reminding him of the closing time. John even invites him as a way of showing friendliness—not that he expects Waylon to accept. John doesn't tell (or even ask Waylon) to leave at the posted closing time. He presents to Waylon an incomplete puzzle that must be interpreted: *for John and his friends to make the game, I must leave the building.* In this indirect way, John communicated his message and avoided disrupting group harmony with a direct statement, which can be perceived as impolite and threatening to group cohesiveness.

Now let's take the same scenario but in a Low Context environment. In the place of Waylon, we have Yankee Waylon with the extra spring in his step.

Yankee Waylon reaches the entrance of his favorite coffee shop and notices another patron more than a few steps behind him. He would have held the door open for her, but she is too far back for that to make any sense.

Waiting in line, Yankee Waylon scans the menu on the wall but decides to stick with his regular favorite. When he's up, he promptly places his order and has payment ready. The barista asks how he's doing and informs him that the two o'clock closing time will be firmly enforced today.

"Usually, we let people linger past the closing time while we clean up, but today we've got the season opener at the ballpark and a crew ready to go. Hope you understand."

"No worries," Yankee Waylon says. "It's a great day for it. Have fun!"

He enjoys his lunch and coffee, then happily hits the sidewalk to begin his wide-open weekend.

Context plays a smaller role in this Low Context environment:

A principle of fairness. Yankee Waylon would have held the door open for the next person behind him if she'd been close enough or needed the help. He's a nice guy too, but it made no sense to delay the process for himself and everyone else for just one person. In absence of a common tradition like Southern Waylon's, a basic principle of fairness is employed.[14] If she'd been closer, he would have held the door without hesitation.

The kindness of efficiency. Low Contexters are not as troubled over group dynamics because their personal identity isn't tied up with group identity. Yankee Waylon felt little to no interest in the group dynamics of near-strangers at the coffee shop as it was mostly irrelevant to his task at hand—namely, to buy his lunch and relax. He felt no compunction to be "polite" in some sort of trivial way, though he was genuinely polite. To Yankee Waylon, conducting his business efficiently and getting out of the way for the next person is how you show kindness in this environment.

A preference for privacy. Small talk about personal matters with strangers is not on the menu for Yankee Waylon. As an I-oriented individual, he feels no pressure to establish (or pretend to establish) deeper connections with people he doesn't know. He reaches out when he feels like it, but there's no cultural pressure to do so. Unwarranted small talk feels like an invasion of privacy to Low Contexters and threatens the prioritized goal of autonomy. Since very little literal meaning is found in the *content* of small talk, its *contextual* possibilities often go unrecognized.

Low Context speech. Barista John clearly and directly let Yankee Waylon know he would have to leave at closing time. He meant nothing harsh by it, and nothing harsh was read into it. It was a matter-of-fact statement that set contractual parameters on the transaction and left no mystery as to its meaning. Low Contexters perceive no threat in direct speech and would argue that it's the best way to communicate.

Conversation between High Contexters requires as much from the listener as it does the speaker.[15] Maybe more. The High Context speaker expects the listener to inherently understand the context and "read between the lines" of what he's saying to discern the full message. It's possible to do this in High Context systems because there's so much shared contextual meaning between speakers and they are accustomed to using it.

When an issue arises between High Context Southerners of the same group, this indirect approach is generally used to solve the problem. Southerners are driven to maintain harmony within their groups, and a direct approach to problems can be interpreted as a confrontation.[16] So instead, the Southerner talks around the issue, expecting the listener to discern what is actually being said and thereby understand the problem. In this system, there's no need to say it all—the listener will put the final pieces in place. When done effectively, the problem is solved without stepping on anyone's toes or resorting to direct confrontation. This, again, is known to the Southerner as "being nice" or "polite," which is important because it supports the harmony of the group. The problem at hand is obviously important too (or else it wouldn't be a problem), but the preservation of group harmony is a higher, ever-present goal.

Not that the goal is always reached. In fact, the indirect approach of "being nice" can sometimes have the opposite effect on relational harmony. When High Contexters use a roundabout, indirect method to address problems, they depend on the listener to correctly and fully interpret the actual message. If this doesn't happen, serious interpersonal misunderstandings can arise. Tension and animosity build up if the problem goes unaddressed, leading to a relational powder keg waiting on a spark. Because the bonds between High Contexters of the same group are so strong and protected, members will tolerate significant acrimony with other group members. But when relational bonds are bent too far, the breaking can be explosive and devastating to the relationship.[17]

Consider a Low Contexter's approach to interpersonal problem solving. They would likely be direct and explicitly say what they want to communicate. This doesn't mean they're insensitive or brash, just more straightforward. The Low Contexter will usually go right at a problem and tell you everything they want you to know about their position. This sets parameters on the conversation and excludes most unspoken, contextual factors. With their concerns so directly stated, the conversation advances on solid, contract-like footing. The listener clearly understands the speaker's position and is able to address the issues directly—no inferences are required. If conflict does arise, the Low Contexter will likely address it at that time rather than later.

Individuals aren't necessarily like the larger culture to which they belong. In fact, some people are quite the opposite and find a big part of their identity in being different than the norm. Furthermore, individuals and cultures can exhibit Higher and Lower Context qualities at different times.[18] It's a messy study, like its subject, but sociologists affix one label or another when that type becomes the majority of the population who establish cultural norms. (Even within these broad categories, there are many other ways to subdivide the behavioral norms of human cultures. We'll address that further in Chapter Six.)

Americans are seen as having a very Low Context culture. Southerners appear to be an exception, displaying characteristics that place them on the High Context side of the spectrum. But as individuals, we all move around the spectrum according to environment and situation.

Low Context Americans are not without High Context qualities. In the privacy of home and with family, there is much that has shared meaning. The same is likely true, though to a lesser degree, when at work. In these situations, they tend to migrate across the spectrum (if only by degrees) toward Higher Context communication. The High Context Southerner will also exhibit Higher or Lower Context behavior in different environments. This is true for all of us.

Not only do we all move around the context spectrum depending on our situation, but we also ascribe different meanings to received communications as we do so. For example, the behavior and language of a football fan rooting for his team in a big game is mostly acceptable, even when it reaches fanatic levels. Transport this behavior to the book club's roundtable and the sports fanatic's boisterous cheers suddenly make him a socially-derided lunatic. Or compare the bawdy language often found in a barroom to what is acceptable in a church. Both environments can lead its participants closer to truth but typically not if the language and behavior of one venue is transposed on the other. Members of both High and Low Context cultures understand that singing the "Fly Eagles Fly" fight song in church is inappropriate (at least outside of Philadelphia). The setting and situation (church and worship) are strong cultural indicators of what kind of enthusiasm is socially acceptable: church is church, play comes later. The same could be said of a work setting.

Church and work are easy examples of settings that have clear limitations on behavior. High and Low Contexters alike agree on the existence of these unspoken boundaries.

(Of course there is variation here too. A fiery revival allows for a different kind of worship than a staid Episcopalian service. In a work setting, a high-pressure restaurant allows different kinds of speech than a library.) But for High Contexters with many relational circles, the limitations and freedoms of most every group setting are as clear as those found in our generic "church" and "work" environments. These norms can vary widely from group to group, but that is no problem for group members. They understand, or will be made to understand, the boundaries of any group to which they belong.

As High(er) Context communicators, Southerners are always (consciously or not) looking for meaning in context. It may not always be there, and of course not everyone shares the same experiences and filters, but context is always part of the discussion.

Intertwined with this perspective is the Southern propensity toward developing and maintaining membership in many different relational circles. Their closest circles are likely where you'll find most of a Southerner's identity, but all social groups play an important part of self-definition. Each of these groups can carry their own specific cultural expectations and contextual meanings, becoming something like "micro cultures." In effect, one's various group memberships each come with their own contextual language, whether or not it's ever verbalized.

It is not surprising that newcomers, and especially Low Context communicators, have a difficult time understanding some of the behavior of High Context Southerners. Here's what they're up against: (1) a culture that strongly emphasizes unspoken, context-driven communication, where (2) the contextual meanings—the stuff being communicated—change according to setting and situation in (3) a society that encourages the development of many relationships and group memberships, greatly multiplying the possibilities and varieties of these "micro cultures."

Southerners are sometimes seen by Low Contexters as having an unstable or changing personality. They see this behavior as evidence of insincerity or lack of personal integrity. But Southerners aren't trying to fool the outsider nor are they without integrity—their social world is just more complex. As they move through it, differing groups and contexts require them to engage and behave accordingly. They do this without thinking about it much because their group-orientated perspective motivates them to account for the group in front of them. They see themselves as behaving appropriately for each group context, but Low Contexters see instead a vacillating personality and wonder which traits are real and which are transient. The answer is that they are all real, depending on the context.

The Low Contexter values consistency of personality across contexts and situations. They may not always *be* consistent, but their culture motivates them to present themselves as such. With their I-oriented perspective, the integrity of the individual far outweighs the needs and integrity of the group. This leads them to speak and behave in ways consistent with their personality or feelings, regardless of context. Southerners often interpret this as rude, brash, or selfish because of the perceived violation of group integrity. And it may be rude to the Southerner, but Low Contexters value their self-integrity too highly to care.

Southerners would say the difference between the cultural styles is politeness and lack thereof. Low Contexters would say it's a matter of authenticity versus superficiality.

As long as everyone is playing by the same rules, both perspectives work just fine. But when interpersonal exchanges are driven by two different sets of rules, misunderstandings abound. The way to overcome this is by understanding first the rules *you* are playing by, and then the rules of others.

CHAPTER FOUR

Mind Your Face

Face-saving is found everywhere in human interaction and perhaps for good reason. Most of us are very concerned about how others see us (and how we see ourselves), so we spend a lot of time managing and cultivating our image. We lie to save face—a lot,[1] suggesting that "face" can outrank the moral taboo on mendacity. (Maybe they're just little white lies, but maybe not.) Why do we do it? Our very identity and status in society are at stake, and we vigorously defend these in many ways.

Maybe you've laughed at a joke you didn't get so you wouldn't appear dim-witted. Or covered for a forgotten birthday with last-minute flowers and chocolate. Or maybe you blame your farts on the dog. (It's a complex world, with many face-saving opportunities.)

Face-saving is frequently employed wherever maturing adults are found playing organized sports. On any given game day in the adult softball leagues, you're likely to see someone like Frank. Frank is the guy who was once a decent athlete but is now more of a foodie and bourbon aficionado. These more recently developed characteristics work against his former physical prowess. After warming up with a favorite summertime lager, he takes his position in the field. Soon, a fly ball comes his way and Frank turns on the afterburners in pursuit. Unfortunately, his afterburners flame out, and he stumbles into a crash.

Then, the magic happens—the magic of face-saving.

Frank goes back to where he fell, searching for something in the grass. Judging from his furious cleat work and stomping of the ground, he has found the culprit. He nods knowingly at what would appear to be a divot in the turf, kicking dirt around to smooth it over. (These mysterious tripping agents have also been spotted on the basketball courts of many community recreation centers, though their remedy is more difficult to discern.)

We don't just save face for ourselves. We save face for others, too.

Imagine a coworker drops the ball by not delivering promised documents to an important client. You happen to be in the office and receive the client's perturbed phone call about the missing work. With profuse apology, you guarantee the documents will be delivered immediately. The coworker is out of the office working with another client. In fact, he is overworked right now and you understand how the mistake could happen. You call him up and learn the work is completed but that he must have forgotten to send it. So you pull it off his computer, call a courier, and send it away. You contact the client and let them know it's en route, blaming the oversight on a recent software change. You decide there's no reason to tell your boss.

Why might you be motivated to save your colleague's face? The health and reputation of the company affects your prospects, no matter who made the mistake. Perhaps, you trained this person and feel your reputation is affected by his success or failure. Maybe you like and value your colleague and want to protect his place in the office. Or, because he has been overburdened for months, you understand how the mistake was made and are sympathetic to his situation.

We act quickly to save face for loved ones. Think of an elderly relative, perhaps a beloved grandmother who is beginning to show signs of dementia. Perhaps she'd always been a very organized person with a keen intellect, but her disease is robbing her of both qualities. Most of us would try to protect her by checking on her more regularly, enlisting help, or even moving her somewhere safe. But we do much more. We don't point out that she has repeated the same question several times. Or that she has spoiled milk in the refrigerator. Or that her socks don't match. We just answer the question again, throw out the milk, and compliment her dress. To draw attention to these mental slips would only hurt her feelings and self-image at a vulnerable time in her life. We protect her because we love her.

These are examples of face-saving in fairly innocuous, everyday forms. But this ubiquitous behavior permeates all levels of human society. When things go badly in companies, organizations or governments, the cycles of blame and face-saving can go on for decades. Who is to blame for economic crashes, legislative failures, or unprofitable ventures?

"Not me" is the most common reply. This blame-shifting saves face as well as other cherished parts of our metaphorical anatomy.

More than *saving* face, we also spend a lot of time *building* face. That can mean different things for different people.

Some people present themselves as adventurous and worldly by telling stories of exotic vacations. Some insist their expensive car or designer handbag is proof of higher status. Some people show us how good they are (or want to be) by wearing religious symbols and putting their name on every church volunteer sheet. Some show us how bad they are by dressing like outlaws, riding a mean-sounding motorcycle, and scowling at children.

The fact is most people work hard to craft their image in the eyes of others. We *need* to be perceived in a way that reinforces who we are, or believe ourselves to be. But we don't make that determination alone. Others validate, modify, or repudiate our desired social image and play an equal part in shaping it both in the eyes of society and within ourselves. In this exchange between our *projected* self-image and the *perceived* image others have of us, our social image—or face—is forged.[2]

Face is a psychological image of a person that develops within social groups of any size.[3] Funny, smart, aggressive, thoughtful, careless, reckless, organized, efficient, et cetera. We use these kinds of words to describe all people, bringing together a full composite of adjectives to create a person's social image. Related to face are words like reputation, respect, integrity, honor, self-image, and prestige.

This meaning for face was taken into English from Chinese during England's long association with Hong Kong. The Chinese have about 100 words or compound words to describe the different types of social "face."[4] In English, there are about five, but the rise of social media has given us the aptly named "Facebook," where face*work* is on ready display. A constant honing of image, reputation, and prestige is a major activity—if not the primary activity—of Facebook's users.

Determining one's face begins with an individual's projection of themselves into relational situations. Others play an equally important role by supporting, modifying, or rejecting that image. It's a very fluid, give-and-take process that is constantly recalibrating our social image over the course of our lives.

As we all know, society's judgments and categories don't always match our own opinions of ourselves. We want the social face that corresponds with who we think we are or who we want to be. Most of us are highly sensitive to situations in which we feel our social face has been besmirched, and losing face is something we strenuously avoid. On the other hand, when someone else enhances our social face we are grateful for the support of our self-image.

Some say they don't play the "face" game—they aren't projecting any image of themselves into society. They simply are who they are: bulwarks of straight-forward integrity and the embodiment of "what you see is what you get." Those who feel this way *are showing concern* for their social face—they want everyone to understand them a certain way. To call them wishy-washy phonies would be a major insult, and they would likely put up a strong defense against this challenge to their social image. This concern for face occurs everywhere that people get together, nearly all the time.

The business of saving or building face—called *face-work*—is central to human interaction and interpersonal communication. But we're not all working toward the same ends or playing by the same rules. There are differences in *whose* face we're motivated to protect, *how* we go about protecting it, and *why* it matters in the first place.[5]

There are many different kinds of people in the world who comfortably identify with different values and interests. We see them all around us: the upstanding citizen, the punk rocker, the health-focused athlete, among many others. These various self-identities are individual products of personality, experience, and circumstance. The owners of the self-identity are certainly concerned with its condition and so must actively maintain it in society's eyes (including their own). The rocker has to rock, the athlete must jog, and the upstanding citizen has to do his part for the community. It's who they are, and their actions back this up. (Of course, one person can be all three: a jogging rocker who does right by his neighbors.)

Beyond the variations of personal identity, you find variation in *how* we support our self-image. The punk rocker and the athlete may not have many common interests, but if they're from the same culture, there's a good chance their facework needs and style are very much shared. Conversely, the punk rockers of New York and Tokyo may enjoy the same music and fashion sense, but the facework styles used to facilitate this self-image are fundamentally different.

High and Low Context cultures produce contrasting psychological needs related to face, which result in very different facework styles.[6] This is why understanding the facework of other cultures is critical to successful cross-cultural communication. To build good relations, we must understand what is important to the other party's "face" and how best to deal with it. We can easily offend people with different cultural norms and not realize our transgression. That doesn't mean we're excused. It means we're culturally unaware and will likely struggle because of it.

FACEWORK STYLES OF HIGH AND LOW CONTEXT CULTURES

The broad classifications of High and Low Context cultures provide key insight into the facework behavior of other people. It was proposed in Chapter Three that the American South is on the High Context side of the spectrum. This is in a country that is widely considered to be very Low Context in nature. Because High and Low Context cultures do facework differently—with different concerns and needs—misunderstandings of meaning and intention arise easily and can derail relationships.

Cultural norms determine what is appropriate, preferred, or required regarding facework, and understanding these dynamics is central to facilitating positive cross-cultural interactions. To this end, we turn to the Face Negotiation Theory of a preeminent scholar in the field, sociologist Stella Ting-Toomey. Our exploration in this chapter relies heavily on her extensive body of work and that of her colleagues. However, this chapter does not represent the totality or intricacies of their theories, but humbly applies them in our mission to discover the nature of Southern culture.

Facework is like a negotiation between two or more people that determines the face status of all involved. If the negotiators have different concerns and needs—and this isn't understood—then a successful negotiation isn't likely. High and Low Context cultures exhibit two fundamental differences in their needs and concerns regarding face:[7]

1. High Contexters are primarily concerned with the face of *others* or are *mutually* concerned for all parties. Low Contexters are primarily concerned with *self*-face.

2. The facework of High Contexters is more focused on securing *group inclusion* and *interdependence*. Low Context facework is more focused on achieving *personal autonomy* and *privacy*.

That being said, there is no single way we behave all the time. This applies to most every human characteristic. Sometimes we're generous, other times we're tight-fisted. Sometimes we're friendly, other times rude. Honest or lying. Brave or cowardly. Emotionally available or not. We are a contradictory lot when it comes to our behaviors and motivations. We are complex.

Our facework behavior is complex as well. Both High and Low Context cultures motivate their members to use facework that supports their autonomy, inclusion to groups, and competency.[8] We all want some degree of personal freedom, meaningful social connections, and a reputation for being capable. Our culture, however, defines preferences and tendencies regarding facework, making some needs more important than others. As Ting-Toomey tells us, these become more apparent in "uncertainty situations," like when we're embarrassed, asking for or complaining about something, or tangled in conflict.[9] The summary below of High and Low Context facework reveals some broad behavioral contrasts.

Principal facework qualities of High Contexters include:[10]

- An emphasis on the "We" identity that drives face concerns for others or mutually for all;
- Inclusion and association as prioritized goals;
- An indirect speaking style with accommodating or avoidance strategies;
- Accounting for subjective factors in problem solving;
- A collaborative approach.

These cultural tendencies can all be traced to the group-focused, We-oriented perspective of the High Contexter. Ting-Toomey holds that facework in High Context cultures can involve the "multiple faces of relatives, friends and family members that are closely linked" to the negotiator, regardless of their presence.[11] High Contexters support and defend other group members because their own self-identity derives from the group as a whole. Driven to maintain group harmony and ensure group cohesion, an indirect speaking style becomes the safe and flexible way to express oneself. The High Contexter also tends to use smoothing or camouflaging strategies in uncertainty situations and may altogether avoid these situations if group harmony is threatened. This indirect, accommodating style of interaction allows for changing conditions and other subjective concerns to be answered. The result is a collaborative approach to facework that helps secure group integrity. But, when everyone's subjective concerns are taken into account, decisions or solutions can reflect a non-linear pattern of logic. In other words, High Contexters tend to prioritize subjective facework concerns over objective solutions.

Principal facework qualities of Low Contexters include:[12]

- An emphasis on an "I" identity that drives self-face concern;
- Autonomy and privacy as prioritized goals;
- A direct speaking style with confrontational or controlling strategies;
- A focus on objective, task-based problem solving;
- A competitive approach.

These Low Context characteristics reveal how the I-orientation expresses its facework needs and concerns. Because self-identity is internally derived and independent of the group, the facework is limited to serving the individual. Autonomy and privacy are prioritized as they secure self-identity and self-determination. To protect autonomy, Low Contexters tend to express feelings and opinions directly—there can be no mistake regarding where they stand. If autonomy is threatened, a confrontational or controlling style of facework is often employed to secure it, giving rise to a more competitive environment. In competitive uncertainty situations, task-focused solutions outweigh the subjective concerns of other people, promoting a linear-logic pattern as the cultural norm.

To illustrate these contrasting styles, consider this hypothetical situation. A few coworkers go for a drink after work. The newest employee (only five months in) asks a question about a specific work-related task. Unfortunately for him, the answer is something he should have known after his first week, and his ignorance indicates the job isn't being done correctly.

In a High Context environment, others would likely move to camouflage and smooth over his mistake. Perhaps someone hushes him and changes the subject, pulling him aside later with whispered assurances that they'll go over it together in private when they return to work. Or someone may announce to the group, "I used to have the same problem. I'll show you how to do it on Monday." This is collaborative facework done to save face for another person in danger of appearing incompetent. This action maintains group harmony and will solve the problem as long as he *is* shown the way on Monday.

It could go poorly if the group completely avoids his question to sidestep the issue of his obvious incompetence. To save him from embarrassment, they might behave as if the question wasn't asked at all. His High Context mind might perceive the avoidance strategy and become more anxious than ever about his deficiency. Standing on dangerous ground, he may not seek help and ultimately leave the problem unsolved.

In a Low Context environment, however, co-workers who hear the embarrassing question will likely take a different tack. They may respond good-naturedly and help-fully: "What?! Who trained you? Get over here and let me tell you about it." This response is very direct but not nec-essarily harsh, especially in a Low Context environment. The problem is simple, as is its task-focused solution: a direct and full explanation of how to do the work. Once properly informed, there is no issue of incompetence and the job can be accomplished properly.

The outcome above is positive for everyone involved, but it could go badly in a less helpful, more competitive environment. "What?! How are you getting anything done if you don't know that! Good luck to you, sir. Your fu-ture with the company is bright." This sarcastic ridicule is clearly an attack and serves to place the attacker above the new employee. There is no concern for group harmony here, and this competitive animosity can undermine the combined efforts of the entire office.

If facework styles are mixed, misunderstandings and problems can follow. Let's say our High Contexter asks the question and the good-natured, helpful Low Contex-ter playfully upbraids him before helping him out. The questioner may be so embarrassed by the broadcast of his ignorance that he feels hurt and betrayed by the one who is trying to help him. Reversing the situation, a High Con-texter may dance around or avoid the question to save face for the forthright Low Contexter who just wants his ques-tion answered and can't understand why it's being avoided. He's unlikely to see that the High Contexter is protecting him in his own way, by his own standard of face-saving.

A key difference between High and Low Context cul-tures has to do with how much importance is placed on facework itself. Because Low Contexters find self-identity from within, they are less concerned about the input of others and more concerned with securing their autonomous self. This becomes the focus of their facework. Within the security of their autonomy, they are free to focus on personal goals and desires.[13] High Contexters generally place greater importance on facework because their self-identities are associated with close groups. Their focus becomes the maintenance of group harmony through supportive facework of others in the group. In this interlocked relational perspective, the self is never fully free from the boundaries of the group. Duty and obligation to social roles makes High Context facework a reciprocal, collaborative process.[14]

Listed below are four additional pairs of Ting-Toomey's ideas about facework that have been selected (cherry-picked, if you will) for their relevancy to Low Contexters adjusting to life in the American South. Keep in mind that these are general qualities that represent the further ends of the High/Low Context spectrum. Most people and cultures represent degrees of these qualities:

- In High Context cultures, the *adaptability* of self-presentation is of key importance in facework.
- In Low Context cultures, *authenticity* of self-presentation style is a key facework concern.[15]
- For High Contexters in conflict, indirect or subtle face negotiation is the polite, tactful approach that maintains group harmony. The direct handling of conflict is viewed as distasteful and impolite.

- Low Contexters in conflict view a more direct face negotiation style as the honest approach that is frank but also fair. They see the indirect approach as cowardly.[16]
- For High Contexters, face negotiations are long-developed and long-remembered.
- Low Contexters tend to negotiate face in the moment using a cost/benefit approach that is shorter lived and not as accumulative as in High Context systems.[17]
- In conflict, High Contexters tend to conflate the issue at hand and the person with whom they're in conflict. This can lead to avoidance of both the person and the issue.
- Low Contexters tend to separate the conflict issue from the people involved. This promotes a task-oriented solution style free of pressure to account for the subjective considerations of others.[18]

A Yankee Goes a-Lunchin'

Facework is everywhere around us and, for the most part, comes naturally while we're within our own cultures. Through socialization, we inherently understand facework norms just like any other cultural norm we grew up with. But when we mix cultural types between High and Low Context systems, the nuances and complexities of facework moves and countermoves are less obvious.

Consider this example of poorly handled facework between a High Context Southerner and a Low Context Northerner (who shouldn't be considered as archetypical, but, rather, illustrative):

A Yankee named Richard nears the end of a business trip down South where he's been working with Harold, a life-long Southerner. The two finish their work after a long morning and go out for a celebratory send-off and lunch at one of Harold's favorite restaurants. Dining out is a serious hobby of Richard's. He's a name-dropper of famous restaurants he's visited and quick to critique any wine list. In his element and eager to evaluate Harold's idea of a "good" restaurant, Richard takes a confident stride to their table.

The waiter, Tom, approaches to greet the men and tell them the day's specials. He arrives to find Richard telling a story about a restaurant in Rome while also furiously perusing the wine list. Richard doesn't acknowledge Tom or allow him a moment to speak, so the waiter walks away to give them some time before trying again. On his return, Tom is still a few paces away when Richard's impatient gesticulations signal he is ready to engage.

"I'll take the chenin blanc," Richard blurts out before Tom even reaches the table. Tom is immediately put off by what he would consider Richard's lack of grace or proper form. It feels like hostility. Tom wants to tell them about the specials of the day, including a very good deal on a fine bottle of wine. Given his first impression, he'd be happy to leave Richard in the dark on this, but Tom knows Harold as a beloved regular.

"Okay, sir. One glass of our chenin blanc. And Harold, how are you today?"

"Great, thanks Tom. Glad to be here." Smiling widely, he does indeed look happy to be there.

"Glad to have you back. We got another case of the Rhone red you liked so much"— Harold smiles again—"and we've got an open bottle of vintage Champagne a rep is trying to sell us. If you want to start with some bubbles, it's beautiful and I've got a couple of glasses left."

"Ahh, you are too good to me. I'll start with the Champagne and move onto the Rhone afterward. Richard?"

"Uh, yeah. Absolutely. Sounds great—change my order. How about some appetizers? I'm starving," he barks into the menu. "Let's start with the clams and something else. You pick."

Harold knows that good things come to those who wait, so he looks to Tom. "I do have something off menu you might like," the waiter says. He describes the dish, which Harold orders. Then, as a quiet aside, Tom clarifies a perceived dilemma with the clams: "Shellfish allergy, right?"

"Yes indeed—you have a good memory. Richard, I don't do shellfish, but I'm told the clams are very good, so you should have them." They work this out and move through their meals. Second glasses of wine are delivered, and the men await entrees.

This is taking too long for Richard, who addresses the issue with Tom on his next trip through. "How's lunch coming along?"

"I'm sure it's almost ready, sir. I'll go check on it now." Tom leaves the table to pretend he's checking with the kitchen. He knows they are working on it, and the wait hasn't been unreasonably long.

"I think that's the mark of a really polished restaurant," Richard says after Tom leaves. "When the courses just roll out one behind the other. One plate magically disappears and another one immediately replaces it."

"Well," Harold counters, "maybe we do things a little different down here." He says this with another smile. "You'll have to adjust a little, but I'm sure you can get the hang of it."

"Don't get me wrong. Everything's been great, but it's that seamless service I'm talking about. You only find that in great restaurant cities."

"Well, maybe so. Sometimes you just gotta roll with it, Richard. We're in no hurry. We finished our work, and now we're drinking some great wine. The food will be here in a minute, I'm sure. Ahh—here it is now."

A few minutes after delivering their entrees, Tom returns to check on the diners. "How is lunch, gentlemen?" Richard holds up a hand as if to say they don't need anything. He's enjoying his meal very much but is too busy between bites telling Harold of how the same dish was prepared for him at a restaurant in Singapore to bother making conversation with the waiter as well. Tom reads this brush-off as displeasure with the meal and worries about Richard's experience. But this was only for Harold's sake. He hopes never to see Richard again.

Harold, without interrupting Richard, smiles and nods his head to Tom. Wordlessly with this motion, he communicates two things which are accurately understood: all is well, and please forgive my companion for he knows no better.

In this example, we quickly see how differences in group- versus self-orientation can play out in Southern settings. Richard's cultural background didn't motivate him to connect with strangers, even the one serving him lunch (perhaps especially the one serving him lunch). He felt no compunction to be "polite" or "nice" in the way that Tom's Southern culture prescribes as proper social behavior. Tom has a group-oriented perspective, and Richard's actions threatened the inclusiveness expected from this cultural point of view. Richard wasn't violating the rules of his own culture, but he did violate the rules of the culture he was in.

Of course, not all High Context Southerners would extend Tom the same sense of inclusiveness as Harold. He could be intentionally excluded for any number of reasons with, perhaps, the power difference between waiter and diner being a likely one. However, when High Contexters do exclude others (for whatever reason), the exclusion carries a mutually understood message: "We are not part of the same group." Because self-identities are intertwined within the boundaries of close groups, and because these relational structures order society, the question of who is *in* a group and who is *out* carries primary significance. High Context facework plays a key role in defining these group boundaries within society.

Richard wasn't excluding Tom in this High Context way. His "I"-oriented cultural perspective wouldn't lead him to believe that Tom needed (or even wanted) to be included in any manner outside of the contractual business of waiting on the table. Richard's "exclusion" was exactly as it looked: "I'll do my thing. You do yours." (Naturally, the power difference would be in play with Low Contexters as well.)

Most Southerners would deem Harold's approach to be well-mannered and pro-social. Having established a friendly diner-waiter relationship from previous visits and accumulated good-will, Harold continued to treat Tom with respect and expand on the relationship. The inclusiveness he showed, despite the power differential, opened the door to a mutually beneficial relationship in which Harold is given special care. He obviously considered Tom to be competent in his role, trusting him with wine selections and everything else related to lunch—quite the opposite from Richard, who did his own thing and later complained about the timing of dishes. This face support from the Southerners has gone both ways: Harold feels special and included in the restaurant "family," and Tom is acknowledged as competent and included in Harold's world.

By contrast, Richard entered this High Context environment and presented facework deemed to be rude and anti-social. This behavior is also accumulative and will likely be remembered. He didn't intend to do this and was only playing by his own cultural rules. But all the same, he did. He seems to bring a competitive approach to dining. As a self-proclaimed gourmand and connoisseur of fine wine, he is almost challenging Harold while they are experiencing his restaurant choice. Comments related to "great restaurants" and "great restaurant cities" imply that Harold has brought them to neither.

Richard brings a controlling attitude to the table. It is, perhaps, technically fair since he is the customer and will be made to fulfill his end of the "contract" by paying the bill. But Harold doesn't like this just as he doesn't like Richard's competitive attitude. It seems uncouth and petty. But, rather than confront Richard, he mostly avoids the issue. The closest he comes is to offer some gentle advice about relaxing and enjoying the afternoon.

In Richard's mind, great restaurants do things a certain way. This inflexible approach is likely to set him up for disappointment. The same can be said of cultures. If we believe our way is the best (or only) way, we're likely to miss out on the hidden gems, like an open bottle of off-menu Champagne. Richard—and all of us—do better when we take cross-cultural opportunities to see how others experience life. That begins with accepting the legitimacy of other cultural norms and perhaps ends with a higher understanding of life itself.

Facework is essential to successful cross-cultural interactions in the American South. While High and Low Context cultures each have their own legitimate rules and norms, its significance to High Contexters is much greater and more prominent in social exchanges. The Southern facework style displays two fundamental aspects of their culture: the group is the primary social unit, and collaboration among group members is the preferred mode of social interaction.

CHAPTER FIVE

Speak Your Mind... or Don't

A Chattanoogan named Jed takes a business trip to Portland, Maine. His company's sister office is undergoing a system-wide software change, and Jed is there to lend his expertise. His hosts are very friendly, picking him up at the airport and taking him out for an early dinner. Afterward, they drop him off at his hotel and bid him goodnight.

The first morning goes well until Jed realizes he's famished at an early hour. He'd skipped breakfast, as he often does, and his mid-morning snack and soon-to-follow early lunch are not on the schedule. All the introductions and planning had taken a lot of energy, and he needs to eat soon. So, he goes in search of that great giver of mid-morning, office-building sustenance: the vending machine.

Jed excuses himself from the large oak table in the meeting room where they work. This is their war room, and about a dozen IT staff have positioned themselves around it. He sets off toward the restrooms because it's the only other area he knows, and along the way he searches for a snack machine. Luckily, he comes across an employee leaving her cubicle.

"Hey, how are you?" he says smiling, obviously wanting to engage.

"I'm fine, thanks. And you?" she replies, matter of factly.

"I'm wondering if you have a vending machine on this floor?"

"Down the hall, to the left. Can't miss it."

"Great," he says, gushing with hope of relief from his hunger. "Thanks so much. Say, when do you usually take lunch around here."

"Whenever you decide, I guess."

Jed settles on a pastry and gets a cup of coffee before returning to the meeting room. These hold his hunger at bay while the room slowly empties and the lunching hour nears. His hosts indicated last night they'd take him out, and he's hoping they will do so in the very near future. An hour passes. Jed's anticipation runs high as his pastry and coffee have failed him.

The room finally dwindles down to the principals in charge, and the talk has turned from the technical task at hand to less pressing matters like where to get quality hockey sticks *and* maple syrup in the same place. Or, at least, that's the conversation Jed imagines through his hungry haze. He decides he's been polite long enough and now must *force* his hosts to move toward lunch. "Whew," he says, kicking back in his chair while looking at them, "I skipped breakfast this morning." Then silence. They look at him and process the information, but they're unclear as to why he told them this. Five, then ten minutes pass and still there is no discussion of lunch. Jed is beginning to feel awful and decides he'll have to be crystal clear about this.

"Y'all have to tell me where to go for breakfast tomorrow," he says with a near-exasperated tone of voice and pleading eyes. "Skipping breakfast was the worst decision I made today."

"Try Billy's Bagels around the corner from your hotel," one of them offers. "Great bagel sandwiches."

A few more minutes pass. Jed is now squirming and beginning to fume. He believes they're ignoring his needs despite the fact that he's clearly presented them. The morning's work is finished, and yet they linger. He finally has enough and stands up.

"All right," he declares with boiled-over annoyance. "Y'all can sit here all day, but I'm going to find something to eat."

As he collects his coat and belongings, his hosts tell him to hold up and they'll all go as planned. They didn't realize he was so hungry. He should've told them, they say. He says he did, but everyone else agrees that he definitely did not. They laugh it off and go to lunch.

Jed did tell them, but in a very indirect manner. To him, his position was clearly stated several times. However, his hosts didn't understand these as statements of action. Being direct speakers, they expected him to be explicit about his need to eat, especially if the need was so great.

These contrasting styles of speech—indirect versus direct—broadly define the communication strategies of High and Low Context cultures.

Indirect Speech Strategies in Southern Conversation

Indirect speech avoids a direct expression of the speaker's meaning or feelings and instead employs a roundabout approach that the listener must interpret to fully understand.[1] Cultural context, body language, and situational information assist indirect speakers in communicating their intended meaning. It falls to the listener to put all these pieces together and correctly interpret the indirect, High Context message.

Low Context cultures value direct speech and encourage members to speak their minds, regardless of potential damage to group harmony.[2] Everything a direct speaker wants to communicate is explicitly spoken, ideally with fullness and clarity. Remember that context plays a much smaller role in the interpersonal communication of Low Contexters.

As an example, an indirect speaker might say "Boy, it sure is chilly tonight," whereas a direct speaker would say "I'm cold. Will you please close the door?" The direct speaker has made his feelings and desires perfectly clear. Not so for the indirect speaker. He has merely made a statement of subjective observation that requires interpretation. He expects the listener to take his meaning and close the door.[3]

Indirect speech is everywhere in Southern communication. You will find it in the mundane banter of daily life or in highly charged interpersonal conflicts. It is, perhaps, a defining characteristic of the Southern humorist, who knows the most profound sentiments are made most clear and truthful when buried in contextual meanings and outright fabrications. It's not difficult to see how Low Context speakers struggle in these environments, and it seems that many problems between Southerners and non-Southerners are related to miscommunication arising from the gap between indirect and direct speaking styles.

The stakes are highest in uncertainty situations like requests, complaints, or embarrassments. It is here that the ability to correctly decipher indirect communication is most highly rewarded, and the failure to do so is most cruelly punished. Many newcomers struggle out of the gate in these situations, but understanding the Southern archetype offers potential remedies.

ASKING FOR HELP

A direct request can seem like a command to the High Context Southerner. Most of us don't enjoy being commanded to action, but because the Southerner feels duty-bound to group members and group goals, saying "no" can be very difficult. "No" involves some level of personal repudiation of the one making the request, which can damage the relationship. This is a danger zone for both parties.

So instead of directly asking for something, the Southerner will often bury the request in vague statements and expect the listener to discern his actual meaning. Consider this hypothetical situation:

Virgil purchases a playground set that was advertised on the office bulletin board. He recently bought a new home and would like to install the little playground for his young children to enjoy. All he needs now is a way to haul it to his backyard and set it up. Two problems present themselves: he has no truck, and he could use a hand putting it together. It's Friday, and he still hopes the family will be on the swings this weekend. While sitting at his desk and mulling over his options, his colleague Robert bounces into his office. The two are highly compatible team members who enjoy working together, but their relationship is mostly limited to work.

"Hey bud, how's it going?" Robert says while dropping off some files. "Any weekend plans?"

"Nothing too exciting," Virgil replies. "I'm hoping to get this playground set I bought from Caroline over to my house and put together. There's not much to it, but I don't have a truck." Virgil knows that Robert drives a truck. "I'm thinking of renting one."

Virgil would like to find anyone who could help him achieve his goal of a backyard playground. Robert just happened to come along, but Virgil doesn't want to impose on Robert's weekend, especially at the last minute. So instead of directly asking Robert for a hand, he simply states his dilemma. Robert knows that *Virgil knows* he has a truck. And also that he's good with tools. Robert understands Virgil's statement as a request for help.

Because Virgil doesn't want to damage the relationship by putting Robert out, his request is very indirect. Robert feels no pressure but understands that a member of his group has goals that require assistance. So he can choose to help or not, with no danger of harming the relationship. Should Robert comply, the conversation might go like this:

"You know, I could help you on Sunday if that's not too late," Robert says.

"Oh, wow! That would be fantastic. But I don't want to mess up your weekend."

"No, it's no problem," he replies. "I'll be over on your side of town anyway."

"That's great! Let me know when is good for you and I'll be ready," Virgil says gratefully. "I'll buy lunch and have a beer in the fridge."

Virgil has found a way to get the playground over to his house and installed. Robert will have the reward of helping a fellow group member meet his goals and will likely feel he has someone he can turn to if he needs a hand sometime in the future. This interaction has strengthened their relationship. But what if Robert is unwilling to comply?

Robert's plans for the weekend are all about decompressing from a difficult week at work. His garden needs some tending and there's a little housework to be done, but his main goals are centered around the chaise lounge on his shade-covered back porch. He doesn't want to alter his plans, but then again, Virgil never directly asked him.

"I wish I had the time to help you out, Virgil, but I am covered up this weekend."

"Oh, no worries, Robert," he responds with genuine gratitude for the sentiment. "We'll find a way."

By using an indirect approach, Virgil has made a request of Robert but also left him an easy way out. Robert's sense of group obligation was not directly called upon, so there is no threat to group harmony. Since he can freely choose to help or not, his autonomy isn't threatened either.

If Virgil had directly asked for help, Robert's sense of autonomy (and his decompression weekend) would both be threatened. His sense of obligation would be tweaked and the scenario could look quite different:

"Hey, Robert, any chance you could give me a hand this weekend? I need a truck to move this playground I bought from Caroline over to my house and get it set up."

Robert squirms a little and avoids Virgil's eyes. He would like to help but needs this weekend to himself. It's difficult for him to say no.

"Oh, man. I'd like to help." He pauses, thinking. "Let me get back to you. I've got a lot going on this weekend. Let me check on a couple of things."

"If you can't do it, it's no problem. Just thought you might have some free time."

"Yeah, I'll let you know." Robert does eventually let him know, by text message: "Sorry. Plate full this wknd. Good luck:)."

These two non-compliance outcomes appear much the same. In both cases, Robert told "white lies" and Virgil didn't receive assistance. But concerning their relationship and the harmony of the group, the two outcomes are quite different.

When asked indirectly, Robert felt free to do as he chose. He did so, and life moved on. But when *directly* asked for help, he felt as though he *should* help another group member—he felt obliged to do something he didn't want to do.

If that was true, and he failed to meet that obligation, then he has failed as a good group member. He may question if Virgil had the right to ask him in the first place. After all, it was a last-minute request to help with something none too pressing. He may come to consider Virgil brash and begin to push him out of his work-group environment. In the end, Virgil may have risked corroding the relationship and finding himself on the outside looking in.

If Virgil's need was greater, a direct request would have elevated the importance of receiving it. For example, if his kids were stranded at a community playground at dark and his transportation had failed him, he would probably (and rightly) employ a direct request. Needless to say, Robert, like most anyone, would probably be there to help.

EXPRESSING WANTS AND NEEDS (IN POLITE COMPANY)

Southerners often express self-wants and self-needs through indirect means. Since Higher Context people have a group-oriented perspective, the expression of individual desires can appear selfish.

A couple wake up hungry early on a Saturday morning. While the coffee is brewing, the husband asks the wife which of two remaining muffins she would prefer: blueberry or carrot.

"It doesn't matter to me—whichever one you don't want," she replies. The husband returns to the pantry and studies the muffins. He thought the carrot muffins were superior, so he plates that one for his wife and settles on a blueberry variety for himself.

When finished, the wife remarks, "You know, they were both good, but I think the blueberry is better."

"I liked the carrot more! Why didn't you ask for the blueberry?!" They laugh it off, having learned the cost of treating muffin selection with an indirect approach.

The direct expression of wants can make Southerners feel like they're taking too much privilege for themselves. Being group oriented, they tend to defer their own desires to others and the group as a whole. Their deference and sacrifice is done to preserve group harmony. They also expect, if only unconsciously, this action to eventually benefit themselves. Because they belong to the group, there is an implicit understanding that at times they will benefit from the deference and sacrifice of others.

Higher Contexters *do have and pursue* self-interested goals, but selfishness is still a dirty word in the American South. Behavior that is perceived as purely self-interested is generally met with disapproval, thereby limiting the likelihood of its success. The indirect approach allows High Contexters to communicate desires without negating the wishes of others, or assuming too much privilege for themselves. The indirect expression of wants is like a trial balloon for Southerners: they send them up in a harmless, indirect manner and see if anyone shoots them down (or politely questions their appropriateness).

Dividing muffins is a low-risk endeavor, but some wants and desires have longer-lasting implications.

A company wins a long-pursued, much-prized contract and must now choose a Project Supervisor to make it happen. Every supervisor there would like the job, and its success would be a feather in the cap of any of their careers. However, most expect it to fall to Pat or Stacy as they have much more experience and expertise than the rest. Both are fully capable, though they bring different strengths to the table.

Pat is elated upon learning she and Stacy are indeed the two finalists for the job, but she is also concerned about how this will affect their working relationship. They were both essential to winning the contract, and both know the other wants to lead it. Pat decides to avoid the potential for competition and let the chips fall where they may.

"I'm going to be happy with whatever you decide," she says to her boss while the two discuss the subject alone. "Just let me know, and I'll be ready either way."

Stacy also avoids direct competition for the job, though she indirectly expresses her desire in a private meeting.

"Either way makes sense to me," Stacy says, "as long as there's good security in place." It so happens that Stacy's specialized knowledge is in security. She has indirectly placed a bid for herself with the premise that security is central to the success of the job.

Another scenario could see one of them *directly* advocate for herself over the other.

"Our profile will skyrocket if we do this right," Stacy tells her boss. "We're entering a new level of business, and if we pull this off, it's a new world for us. But remember, if we don't have security, we don't have anything. Pat is great at what she does, but security makes it all possible."

When Pat got wind that Stacy was advocating herself for the job, she felt she'd been thrown under the bus. The two of them had written the proposal together and lobbied for the contract. No matter who took the lead position, the other would be essential to its success. Pat believes she has been treated unfairly by Stacy, and this could undermine their working relationship.

To directly claim a prize for oneself in a High Context environment is to flirt with disaster. Even if you win the prize, the animosity and hard feelings created can greatly outweigh the victory itself.

COMPLAINTS

Complaints can be difficult to lodge in any culture because you're inherently criticizing or curtailing someone's actions when you do so. For High Contexters, the action and the person associated with the action are very much tied together. The same is true for the criticism and the critic—the two are conflated. Because the issues and people are bound together, Southerners take extra precautions when criticizing the actions of someone else, especially if they're in the same group.

Julie is pleased to have her new neighbors living beside her. They are pleasant, considerate people who have distinguished themselves from the previous occupants by maintaining their lawn and not honking their car horns at all hours of the night. Whereas their college-aged predecessors had been night-owl rock musicians, the new neighbors are early-to-bed, early-to-rise types who seem to appreciate quiet reflection and gentle breezes.

Soon though, a problem arises. Julie begins to regularly smell garbage wafting over her fence and into her lovingly developed patio. Sitting in her patio chair with a book and surrounded by the herbs, flowers, and vines she so carefully selected, the persistence of the stench drives her to action.

She quickly discovers its source. In the thoughtful and fastidious care of their home, her new neighbors have placed their garbage receptacles right next to the privacy fence separating the properties. They likely don't realize how close her patio is to their garbage. Or how profound an effect the July sun is having on it. Thinking the situation over, Julie decides not to criticize them in any way. They've only been here for a month and already she credits them with greatly improving the quality of her life.

After some consideration, a plan is developed.

"Hey, Barbara!" Julie says brightly while standing on a chair and looking over the fence at her neighbor who is inspecting the ash bin of her grill. It is a scorcher of a summer day, and the garbage smell has reached its zenith alongside the thermometer. Julie calls Barbara over to the fence line.

"I'm hosting a little cocktail hour this Friday on the patio if you want to pop over for a bit," Julie says as Barbara approaches the fence. "There will probably be a few more neighborhood people you haven't met. Bring Bob, too."

As Barbara approaches the garbage cans, she finally catches a whiff of the overwhelming stink. "Whooo!" she says, with clearly offended senses. "I didn't realize these were still so bad—the boys must have had a body in there."

"While you're here, check out my patio. The morning glories have really taken off." Julie invites her to walk around the fence. Barbara happily complies, and in doing so, she understands how close Julie's beloved patio is to her own garbage cans. Returning home, she moves the cans away from the fence line and to the top of the cleaning schedule.

The cocktail hour was a success, with no stench, nice cocktails, and warm introductions to new neighbors. There was no threat to group harmony or to the new neighbors' autonomy. It is the way of the High Contexter, though not the only way.

CONFLICT AND ATTACKS

We've seen that High Context cultures tend to dissuade their members from upsetting the harmony of the group. Outright attacks are a clear violation of that rule and can irreparably damage a relationship. Indirect speech can help bridge the gap between the need to express outrage and the cultural prescription to "be polite."

A grandmother takes her two grandchildren to the ballpark for a baseball game. It is a beautiful day, and she is delighted to be there. But unfortunately for her, a manic smart phone user sits right behind her, polluting the air with a steady flow of beeps and obnoxious ring tones.

He diligently (and lamentably) ensures rows six through eight are kept abreast of his social media postings.

By the end of the second inning, Granny is having a hard time ignoring it. At the start of the sixth, the offender's phone rings for the umpteenth time. Granny can stay quiet no longer. But instead of exploding, she does the opposite: she is all sweetness and light.

"That is some kind of cell phone you've got there, Sonny," she says when the call ends.

"Well thank you, ma'am," he says genuinely. "I just got it yesterday!"

"I could tell you like it," she says with a smile as she meets eyes with him. "I've heard it more than I've heard the announcer." She gives forth a good-natured chuckle.

"Yes, ma'am," he says while absorbing her meaning. He responds with some playful acknowledgment of his own: "I think I'll put the phone away for a bit, but let me know if *you* want to play with it."

They share a laugh and move on.

Granny did attack Sonny for diminishing everyone's good time, but it was done in a non-threatening manner. He understood her meaning ("your phone is killing me") and also that she didn't want to offend. He was offered a graceful way out and took it.

EMBARRASSMENT

High Contexters are inclined to save face for others as much as themselves. In embarrassing situations, a typical Southern response would be to avoid it altogether (pretending it doesn't exist) or to talk around it (downplaying its prominence and diverting attention).

A group of twenty-something Southerners gather in Nashville for a college reunion of sorts. Some of them haven't seen each other for a while and are reconnecting.

Others live near each other and have remained close. As they sit in an ice cream parlor and catch up, one of them misuses the word "boondoggle." Everyone else who is listening lets it slide. She repeats it. A couple of them look at each other. When she emphatically misuses it a third time, someone speaks up.

"Honey, I think you're doing that thing again where you misuse a word," one of her friends says gently.

"No! Which one?"

"Boondoggle, honey."

"No way! I know what it means! It means a great day off or vacation—like when a *dog* visits the *boon*docks." She is lightly rebuffed with a dubious look. In defense, she turns to her husband who has been involved in another conversation. "What does *boondoggle* mean?"

He repeats her dead wrong understanding of the word.

"See! I told you!"

They all let it go, and she continues to tell her story, misusing the word "boondoggle" two more times in triumph and with confidence.

In the end, saving face for the malapropist and maintaining the good mood of the gathering outweighed the importance of correcting her misunderstanding. Group harmony and cohesiveness are often more important than being right, especially when a group member is at risk of embarrassment.

These stories illustrate the Southern tendency to employ indirect speech in uncertainty situations where the danger to relational harmony is greatest, but indirect speech isn't limited to these situations. It can be found everywhere in Southern conversation.

THE MEANINGS OF SILENCE, AND THE MALLEABILITY OF TRUTH

A common problem between Southerners and Low Context speakers concerns the role (or, more accurately, roles) of silence. Where Low Contexters tend to view silence as empty space to be filled, High Context Southerners see it as an act of communication that carries meaning.[4] Low Contexters are made uncomfortable and embarrassed by what feels like an interruption to the flow of conversation. High Context Southerners understand silence as part of the conversation and it is rarely considered an interruption.[5]

Silence used in this way is a form of indirect speech and comes with the expectation of an accurate interpretation from the listener. There's little wonder how these two perspectives on silence (uncomfortable void vs. meaningful speech) can lead to problems.

A general sense that "less is more" undergirds the conversational behavior of High Contexters.[6] By sharing a contextual, non-verbal "language," they can minimize what is actually spoken and still fully communicate their message. So when something *is* said, it carries more weight because of its relative scarcity. Within this dynamic, silence is often used like a frame around speech to emphasize its importance to the speaker. "Strong and silent" isn't necessarily an accurate description of the archetype, but the less-is-more approach is familiar and well understood by High Context Southerners.

Silence is often used in the South to indicate embarrassment, disagreement, disapproval, truthfulness,[7] and much more depending on how High Context the environment is. This may seem daunting and frustrating to Low Contexters, making it important to be mindful of the motivations and preferences of High Contexters. Group harmony is a primary goal, and they achieve it by using smoothing and camouflaging strategies, along with wholesale avoidance.

Southerners may feel the pain of an embarrassed group member as much as the one embarrassed. When these situations occur, Southerners often employ the silence of complete avoidance. This takes the pressure off the one embarrassed (a kindness), but it also indirectly communicates that group cohesion is secure. Nothing says "What happened is okay" quite like a total avoidance of the event's existence.

Disagreements pose a risk to group harmony. The risk grows if the disputed positions are conflated with the disputing parties, which is a tendency of High Contexters. To avoid explicit disagreement but still express their position, Southerners will often employ silence. This averts the risk to group harmony but also stands as its own non-verbal statement: I don't agree with you, so I have said nothing to support your speech.

Silence that communicates disapproval is much the same as no support is offered for the other's actions or speech. The difference might be that disapproving silence is communicating a threat of exclusion—a serious matter, since High Contexters depend on group approval and inclusion to anchor identity. The silent treatment is often how Southerners show disapproval. This sends the message without being too explicit, allowing space for the disapproved party to change course and avoid a face-damaging confrontation.

Truthfulness and integrity are important in all cultures. The High Contexter has a tendency to express truthfulness by framing clearly-made statements with stark silence. This punctuating silence invokes the integrity of the speaker and uses it as evidence of honesty. To challenge the integrity of a High Context Southerner is to start a serious conflict, and members of High Context systems know this. So, by using silence to invoke his integrity, the High Contexter makes a strong bid to support his statements as truthful. It doesn't mean they *are* true but indicates that the speaker is presenting his statements as such.

The motivation to protect and promote group harmony is sometimes strong enough to make High Context Southerners misrepresent their own thoughts, feelings, or desires.[8] It may seem strange to equate harmony (or kindness) with dishonesty, but harmony is the intention of the High Contexter who misrepresents himself for the sake of the group.

High Contexters value honesty, but they value keeping relationships even more. "If telling the truth means damaging a relationship, they would rather tell a white lie," social psychologist Harry C. Triandis writes.[9] Low Contexters (who are less sensitive to relational facework) may view this as purely dishonest, even if well intentioned.

Since disagreements are often perceived as more than differing opinions or desires—they can signal a rejection of the one disagreed with—Southerners often take the safer route of just going along. Rather than risk offending another group member, they will misrepresent themselves. This is because group goals and group consensus often outweigh an individual's goals or opinions in a High Context environment.

THE UNCOMMITTED QUALIFIERS OF HIGH CONTEXT SPEECH

Maybe, perhaps, and *probably* are important qualifiers in the language of High Context Southerners.[10] These uncertain and unassertive words promote a type of interaction that allows for group consensus to emerge. No one gets their toes stepped on, and disagreements are minimized.

By remaining non-committal, High Contexters maintain flexibility to adapt their position as the situation changes. The changing contexts of places, events, and people can alter how they are motivated to behave and how they view any one issue. They see this flexibility as expressing different parts of their personality and self, making adaptability an important personal quality. To make this possible, they tend to use uncertain qualifiers (like "maybe") instead of direct, explicit, and affirmative statements. An assertive position is taken only with considerable caution, especially if it challenges group norms or other group members.

By contrast, Low Context speakers tend to employ categorical words like *certainly, absolutely*, and *positively*.[11] Motivated to present themselves authentically, Low Contexters are eager to use these assertive declarations of their thoughts and opinions. Consistency of self-image is rewarded in Low Context cultures, which can lead to confusion when dealing with High Contexters who are rewarded for adapting their selves to many different situations.

Indirect speech is everywhere apparent in Southern culture. It can be as unconscious as the starving Chattanoogan's story, or as overt as Granny's speech to the guy with annoying phone habits. It allows speakers to express their thoughts with less risk of offending others and disrupting group harmony. It also creates flexibility so that changing situations and contexts can be given the appropriate response.

There are, of course, risks to indirect speech. By using ambiguous language, the speaker relies on the listener to infer the full meaning. Mistakes can be made. Furthermore, since High Contexters will sometimes disguise or misrepresent their true feelings or opinions, unaddressed issues can lead to major blow-ups. Though most Southerners are well-versed in the nature and nuances of indirect speech, misunderstandings of meaning or intention are a danger for even the most expert of High Context speakers.

A much riskier endeavor in the South, however, would be to use direct speech exclusively. This approach can come off as arrogant and self-centered since directly assertive statements leave no room for the opinions of others, the consensus of the group, or for changing conditions. As we've seen, High Contexters hold *collaboration* as a cultural norm in conversation, while Low Contexters bring a *competitive* approach to personal interaction. The Low Contexter is ready for his statements to be challenged because the competitive approach invites it as a means to a solution. The High Contexter using a collaborative framework perceives direct challenges as a threat to the group and a violation of face. This isn't to say that challenges aren't made all the time in High Context systems—it's just that they're made in a more indirect, less definitive manner.

Variation is always the norm in social dynamics, and black-and-white thinking won't get you far. Not all members of Low Context systems are always direct, nor are all High Contexters always so indirect. People are different one from another but also display different behavior at different times. High Contexters are often more direct speakers inside the protective bonds of close relationships.[12] This doesn't mean they're as direct as a true blue Low Contexter, but they're *more* direct than they would be in other situations. Conversely, Low Contexters tend to use more High Context speech within their close personal relationships where shared meaning is found through shared lives.

Some people are anomalies to their cultural norms. And most of us can't be described by the extreme ends of the High or Low Context spectrum. Rather, we are located somewhere toward the middle, our own shade of gray.

Wherever we find ourselves along the spectrum, we live within the boundaries and norms of the larger culture surrounding us. Those norms dictate what is accepted as normal communication behavior within society. If we violate them, we usually know we're doing so. When unintentional violations occur, they are typically met with social reprimand, making us abundantly aware of the aberrant behavior.

Though most people identify with the culture in which they were socialized, many others find identity in diverging from mainstream norms. They, too, are strongly affected by the larger culture as it remains the baseline against which they measure themselves as different. Cultural norms and boundaries are deeply embedded in our psyche. We all use them as the standards of measurement to calculate our own place in society—to define (or prove to others) just how close or how far we are from being socially "correct."

Southerners with Low Context sensibilities eventually learn that speaking freely and directly can lead to trouble, pressuring them to modify their innate speaking style when the situation calls for it. Likewise, the High Context Yankee eventually learns that indirect, ambiguous speech often goes unheard, motivating them to use more Low Context speech to match their social environment. However, those who run counter to their culture don't have to sacrifice their true nature just to fit in. They adapt to improve their message and, in the process, expand and sharpen their communication skills. They develop as "bilingual" in both High and Low Context speech and become stronger communicators and leaders because of these developed skills.

Newcomers to the South who discover their innate cultural style violates the norms of their new surroundings will benefit from becoming "bilingual." If our goal is to communicate clearly and effectively, understanding the dominant communication style of our audience greatly improves our chances for success. Doing so doesn't undermine our true nature or internal value system. Rather, it expands our communication skill set and increases our awareness of other cultures, thus opening the door to successful cross-cultural interactions.

CHAPTER SIX

The Southern Collectivist

James and LaKeisha met in a large Northeastern city, fell in love, and married. A few years later, the happy couple moved to the suburbs of the large Southern city that is LaKeisha's hometown. They were excited to leave the more densely populated urban life that brought them together for someplace easier to live, where the people were friendlier, and opportunities were growing.

James had always felt out of sync with his own culture. In high school, he preferred collaborative activities to competitive ones. Rock bands and writing groups went together with volunteer work at the soup kitchen and the animal rescue shelter. As he finished college and grew into his first jobs, he began to more fully understand himself as somehow different from most in his social environment. His natural tendency to cooperate and work with others was a liability in the harsher, more competitive environment that was his working life. There, personal ambition ruled the day, and the arc of one's career would define the person. James was fully aware of these rules and was able to find success. (This was his native culture, after all.) But he still had a very serious problem: it made him unhappy.

The South, he thought, would offer him the chance to live in a friendlier place that better suited his nature. He'd always enjoyed LaKeisha's family and visits to her hometown. Now he would live there and embrace a life interconnected with her family.

He quickly discovered just how closely connected Southern circles can be—and what it means to be a full-fledged member of one. He loved what he thought of as the Big Hug from his new family and embraced his new role as part of a collection of people whose lives intertwined and overlapped. They were in it together, and they meant to win it together.

The duties and obligations required of those inside the Big Hug were many. Though James anticipated and desired an interconnected approach to life, he wasn't quite prepared for how much would be asked of him.

James had been the *most* involved in the lives of family and friends back home, and he was always the one who could be counted on in times of need. But down South and inside the Big Hug, the obligations piled up and made him feel imposed upon. There was the uncle who needed help getting firewood together for older members of the extended family. This uncle procured the wood and seasoned it, but then it had to be cut, delivered, and stacked. James enjoyed the work and liked to be helping the family in such a meaningful way. But then came the dog sitting, the babysitting, transport rides to the family's auto mechanic, the weddings of people they didn't like, the family friend who had knee surgery and needed her yard mowed. The kids' ball games, church on Sundays, a cousin's cross-state move. It never seemed to end.

James reached his breaking point while watching his beloved Mets play October baseball. Everything was set: the den was primed, his favorite beer was on ice, and his Mets jersey remained superstitiously unwashed as it had been since their playoff berth. Just as everything was set for a perfect night, his sister-in-law called for the emergency babysitting of her three-year-old son. His wife, of course, said yes. James and LaKeisha didn't have or plan on having any children. Child-free baseball in October was one of the reasons why, James thought to himself.

After his nephew had left and the Mets had lost, he sat down with LaKeisha and asked for help. Separating from his self-identity of the "most-involved and dependable person" was hard, but he had to secure some level of autonomy. He loved her family but was overwhelmed by it too. This marked the beginning of James taking control of his life again. He eventually found the right balance for himself and was able to manage his personal space while remaining a full member of the Big Hug.

In his home culture, James needed more interconnectivity with people and groups than was the norm. His identity developed around the feeling of being different than the mainstream—more empathetic and involved in the lives of others. However, in his life down South, he needed more autonomy and privacy.

For James, the mainstream cultural norms had changed. Though the transition was difficult, he gained important self-knowledge and came out the other side with a better understanding of his own needs and preferences. The contrast of cultural environments made this possible, empowering him to better manage his life within both.

Empowerment through knowledge is our cross-cultural mission too. To this end, we've explored Hall's ideas about High/Low Context communication, Ting-Toomey's Face Negotiation Theory, and the indirect speech habits of High Contexters. Now we turn to a model that stands as the most referenced and important means of inquiry in cross-cultural psychology: the individualism-collectivism model.[1]

The United States is widely considered by cross-cultural researchers to be the most individualistic country on earth.[2] We love self-made-man (and woman) stories because they highlight the power of the individual. We tend to blame the individual when things go badly and are philosophically inclined toward the idea of personal responsibility. We cherish our individual rights and herald individual achievement.

We are what we are. And we are an individualistic country.

But as we've seen already in these pages, there is something different about the American South. Southern cultural and historical antecedents are unique in the United States. Southerners tend to have a *group*-oriented perspective that meaningfully distinguishes their social behavior from the *individual*-oriented perspective associated with their country. Their communication preferences reflect the concerns and motivations of a We-oriented culture, often confounding those with I-orientations. The result is a United States composed of two distinctive cultural types that don't quite understand they're speaking different languages.

Most Americans are individualists, and this is well documented in the research. Southerners, however, are born of a culture that exhibits clear evidence of collectivism. Used in this context, the terms *individualism* and *collectivism* are not descriptors of political systems, but instead describe cultural systems.[3]

Individualistic cultures promote an archetype that is self-oriented, direct in speech, and competitively focused on individual goals. Collectivistic cultures promote an archetype that is group-focused, careful and indirect in speech, and willing to sacrifice individual goals for larger group goals.

This model overlaps with the High/Low Context model,[4] but the individualism-collectivism framework goes further, encompassing and superseding Hall's ideas about context in communication. Introduced by Dutch researcher Geert Hofstede in his groundbreaking work *Culture's Consequences*, the individualism-collectivism model has become the standard against which all other research in this area is measured.* Hofstede's brief definition of the two cultural types opens our exploration of these ideas:

Individualism pertains to societies in which the ties between individuals are loose: everyone is

---

* Though these concepts had been explored by cultural anthropologists, sociologists and philosophers for a long time, Hofstede's model has dominated academic study in these fields since *Culture's Consequences* was released in 1980.

expected to look after himself or herself and his or her immediate family. *Collectivism* as its opposite pertains to societies in which people from birth onwards are integrated into strong, cohesive in-groups, which throughout people's lifetime continue to protect them in exchange for unquestioning loyalty.[5]

These descriptions represent the far ends of the individualism-collectivism spectrum, but most cultures exhibit only degrees of these qualities, placing them somewhere closer to the middle. For example, researchers find traditional Chinese culture to be very collectivistic relative to other cultures, whereas Argentina is found to be much less so, though still registering on the collectivism side of the spectrum. Likewise, this variation by degrees is found within populations of the *same* culture. We are all a little different from each other. Like James from our story above, some people can be categorized as generally more collectivistic than their *own* culture, but still less so than other cultures (and vice versa).

IN SEARCH OF THE SOUTHERN COLLECTIVIST

The psychological orientation of self—I or We—fundamentally shapes how we perceive and interact with the world. Do we discover our own identities and become responsible for them? Or do we find identity through the connections to our groups, becoming obligated to group needs and goals? Our answers have far-reaching effects on how we approach the world.

Individualists ideally carry a high self-esteem into the world, priming them to competitively seek personal success and fulfillment. Ambition runs strong, and they are ready to fully express their opinions, feelings, and unique qualities to attain personal goals. The collectivist Southerner sees this behavior as brash and self-serving—two qualities deemed to be negative, possibly even immoral. Their "We" focus makes the group more important than individual goals and personal ambition.[6] Southerners are often suspicious of people who toot their own horn too loudly and too often, further exacerbating problems between the two types. (Perhaps this suspicion is well-placed as research has indicated that individualists tend to overestimate their own abilities compared to others.[7])

The Southern collectivist steps out into the world with expectations of polite and collaborative social interactions.[8] Personal ambitions and opinions are often kept quiet in deference to group goals and group harmony.[9] Individualists find this restraint to be cowardly, though the real danger for collectivists is the stifling of their unique personal qualities.

Collectivists are more likely to be influenced by the values and attitudes of their closest group associations.[10] These "in-groups" are maintained and defended because they represent key parts of their identity and validate their place in society. Typically, fellow in-group members are given better treatment than outsiders, and reciprocation is expected when the opportunity is presented. Defining in-group values—in effect, defining *identity*—requires rejecting other values represented by other groups. Sociologists label these "out-groups." The boundaries between in-groups and out-groups in collectivist systems tend to be fixed, difficult to cross, and of substantial social consequence.[11]

Individualists have in-groups and out-groups too, but these have much less impact on behavior—they are neither as fixed nor as important as they are for collectivists.[12] When personal goals shift, or if participation in the group costs more than its benefits, individualists tend to move on, forming new relationships and group associations that are more beneficial to their current goals.[13]

An early example of collectivist in-group/out-group dynamics in the South comes from the Virginia Cavaliers, as presented by the historian David Hackett Fischer. In this case, an eighteenth-century immigrant has been warned about the powerful ruling elite, which was the ultimate Cavalier in-group:

> John Randolph, in speaking of the disposition of Virginians, very freely cautioned us against disobliging or offending any person of note in the colony ... for says he, either by blood or marriage, we are almost all related, and so connected in our interests, that whoever of a stranger presumes to offend any one of us will infallibly find an enemy of the whole. Nor, right or wrong, do we forsake him, till by one means or other his ruin is accomplished.[14]

To offend the interconnected Cavaliers was to court disaster. And you might not even know the disaster had occurred until your ruin was complete.

African American slaves, by nature of the state of bondage and the color of skin, would always represent a special class. They were viewed merely as property and tools of the economy. But, of course, slaves didn't see themselves this way. They saw themselves as we all do: as humans deserving of equal status and rights. Living in a hostile world both before and after emancipation, African Americans in the South would look to their own developing American culture to secure their families and pursue their freedoms. After emancipation, race would endure as a principal factor in determining group association across the South and, indeed, across the country.

Another example of in- or out-group dynamics can be found in the feuding behavior of Southern hillbillies. The Hatfield and McCoy feud famously ignited over the contested ownership of a hog, but the bloody war it became was about family honor and clan loyalty. Honor and loyalty were powerful forces to Americans of Scotch-Irish heritage,[15] and they remain so today. This "culture of honor" is what writer Malcolm Gladwell refers to in his popular book *Outliers*, where he draws a strong connection between these Americans and the borderland culture of north Britain.[16]

Feuding among clans was always a possibility in the mostly lawless American backcountry, much as it had been among the warring clans of the northern English borderlands in the centuries before. Clan inter-reliance was the key to survival and prosperity, and it represented the "We" that was the source of clan members' identity. Backcountry Americans would not shy away from using violence to defend the integrity of their clan.

Fischer writes that clan bonds became stronger over time in Southern Appalachia and quotes an early twentieth-century "mountain woman" describing the interconnections of their clan:

> All the children in the district are related by blood in one degree or another. Our roll-call includes Sally Mary and Cripple John's Mary and Tan's Mary, all bearing the same surname; and there is, besides, Aunt Rose Mary and Mary-Jo, living yon side the creek. . . . [The children] know that Uncle Tan's smokehouse is the resource of all in time of famine; that Aunt Martha's kind and strong hands are always to be depended on when one is really ill; that Uncle Filmore plays the fiddle at all the dances, and Uncle Dave shoes all the mules owned by the tribe.[17]

The culture of these backcountry settlers, like that of their ancestors, depended on the cohesiveness of their clan. They arrived on New World shores as a collectivist culture and their strong group orientation would be reinforced in the tough and contested backcountry of Appalachia. Though modern day "feuds" aren't likely to lead to open gunfights, offenses to individuals are often perceived as offenses to the whole group, leading to festering antagonism from all quarters. This can happen with a neighbor over the fence, a parent from your kid's school, or another department across the office floor.

Collectivists are driven to maintain the integrity of their primary in-groups, and fellow group members often receive special treatment and protection. This impacts reasoning and makes value judgments dependent on who is being scrutinized.[18] This *particularist* mindset, one that accounts for and gives meaning to subjective, contextual factors—like *who* is involved—can result in a non-linear style of reasoning. This means that for the particularist, what is true and right in one context or situation isn't necessarily so in others.

Individualists bring a Low Context approach to social exchanges and tend to view unrelated factors as irrelevant to the matter at hand.[19] Context is delinked from the reasoning process, producing a *universalist* worldview: what is true and right here is also true and right everywhere. This, ideally, translates to a people who apply their value judgments based on what happened, not who was involved. These cultures favor a linear-logic style of reasoning, which is facilitated by the exclusion of subjective and contextual factors.

A major difference between these types involves how public and private settings are perceived.[20] Individualists—as universalists—see little difference between the two settings that could substantially affect a person's self-identity and reasoning process. Ideally, they have a consistent self-image that doesn't change much, and they believe that what is right and true in one place is right and true in every place. Collectivists—as particularists—are more likely to see differences between public and private settings, and this perspective is likely to affect how they reason and interact within them.

The social psychologist and pioneering cross-culturalist Harry C. Triandis points us toward the collectivism of

Japan for an illustration of particularism in public and private settings. "[A]ctions that are inappropriate ... do not worry most Japanese unless the perpetrator is found out and there is public dishonor," he writes.[21] The immorality of the action itself is not a social problem until it threatens the in-group with dishonor and shame. For individualists, an immoral act would be so whether or not there were social consequences. This highlights an interesting difference between collectivists and individualists: the former is more sensitive to shame, where the latter is more sensitive to guilt.[22]

Shame and guilt as repercussions of immorality demonstrate the contrasting self-orientations of "We" and "I." The collectivist is obligated to uphold the integrity of the group and maintain its public face. Shame occurs when one fails to do so, but it doesn't deliver its full punishment unless society discovers it. The individualist is allegiant to internally held principles that are perceived as universally right or wrong. Guilt exists within the individual whether or not there are social repercussions.[23]

The contrasting psychological pathways taken by these cultural types are made clearer by examining the value systems guiding each group. Extreme collectivists most value tradition, family, security, social order, and politeness. Extreme individualists value uniqueness, autonomy, personal achievement, broadminded thinking, and the free expression of personal opinions.[24]

However, most of us aren't so extreme, and we should be careful not to stereotype people of other cultural systems. For example, it would be inaccurate to think of individualists as purely selfish and collectivism as a model of social benevolence.

Collectivists must seek their own self-interests, too, and they can be just as selfish as any individualist. However, they must pursue that self-interest without offending cultural norms. This means they can't *appear* selfish (or exclusively self-interested) and must receive social approval in order to advance their self-serving goals. The possible workarounds are many, but the primary goals of group cohesion and harmony must be respected.

By the same turn, individualism doesn't imply a lack of empathy or an unwillingness to help others. Individualists simply operate under different norms for expressing concern or supporting others in society. Individualist systems promote competition between individuals, and this is often *perceived* by collectivists as shameless self-interest.

The individualism-collectivism model is the broadest, most important, and most widely used tool in the cross-culturalist's bag, but there are other tools and many other ways to describe cultural systems. Hofstede uses five other dimensions alongside individualism-collectivism, which offer more detailed and in-depth descriptions of cultural types. Other researchers and theorists employ entirely unique models. Rather than explore all of these specific ideas, we'll briefly turn to Triandis's simplified model that combines many of them into a comprehensive and more accessible classification system.

Triandis subdivides individualistic and collectivistic cultures into *Vertical* or *Horizontal* types, creating four primary cultural patterns. Vertical systems accept inequalities across society, while Horizontal systems promote equality. This addition to the individualism-collectivism model was introduced as a way to simplify and standardize across the body of work in this area of research. His brief descriptions of each cultural type are presented below, followed by examples of cultures that represent them:[25]

- **Vertical Individualistic**: An autonomous self is assumed. Individuals see themselves as different and independent from others. Inequality is expected and competition is promoted. *Examples: the Northeast United States, England, France.*

- **Horizontal Individualistic**: An autonomous self is assumed. Though individuals see themselves as independent, others are seen as having equal status to themselves. The self is understood to be basically the same as other people. *Examples: Sweden, Australia.*

- **Vertical Collectivistic**: Individuals view the self as a combined aspect of in-groups but also as different from other members, with some having more status. Interdependence anchors self-identity. However, inequality is accepted. Duty and sacrifice for in-groups are important qualities in this type of culture. *Examples: the Southern United States, India.*

- **Horizontal Collectivistic**: Individuals sees themselves as combined parts of in-groups, with all members being very similar and equal to each other. The self is understood as interdependent with in-groups, and equality emerges as the

> essential characteristic of this pattern. *Examples: China, Guatemala, and in monastic traditions.*

The U.S. is understood to be a Vertically Individualistic and Low Context culture: members are self-oriented; different and independent from each other; accepting of inequality; encouraging of competition; and inclined toward using explicit, direct speech.

The American South looks like a Vertically Collectivistic and High Context culture: members are group-oriented; interdependent but different from each other; accepting of inequality; encouraging of sacrifice for the group; and inclined toward using indirect, context-driven speech.

With the Vertical-Horizontal model, we're able to distinguish between the Horizontally Collectivistic cultures of Asia and the Vertically Collectivistic culture of the American South. These cultures share a group-oriented perspective and favor High Context speech. However, in the Horizontal Collectivism found in East Asian cultures, people are seen as basically equal in status to each other. This perspective is made clear in a proverb ascribed to traditional Japanese culture: "The nail that sticks out gets hammered down."[26] In the American South, you find a very different outlook:

> [Southerners] carry in their hearts or genes or livers or lights an ancient, God-credited belief that a man has a right to do as he pleases. A right to be let alone in whatever plain of triumph he has staked out and won for his own. A right to go to hell or climb to the stars or sit still and do

nothing, just as he damn well pleases, without restraint from anybody else and most assuredly without interference from any government anywhere.

–Arkansan and *New York Times* journalist Roy Reed, as quoted by sociologist John Shelton Reed (1976)[27]

This fierce insistence on one's own individual freedom, while at the same time accepting that others aren't as free, could be expected from a Vertically Collective society. It is *their* group that matters—others must fend for themselves in a world of inequalities.

It was a hallmark of the warring clans of Britain's borderlands and their Scotch-Irish descendants in the American backcountry. They held their freedoms in high esteem, but the clan's interests would always supersede the needs of individuals within the clan and, certainly, without.

Likewise, the landed Cavaliers of the Chesapeake (and their aristocratic descendants) strongly believed in their own individual freedoms but were more than willing to take those freedoms away from others. They saw themselves, their families, servants, and slaves as a collective "We," but inequalities between these members were understood as facts of life. This was much as it had been in seventeenth-century southwest England.

Surviving the horrors of slavery would bind together many of its victims into a collective understanding of "We," one based on a common skin color and terrifying dilemma. The mother cultures of West Africa endowed the slaves with a collectivist's perspective, and there could be no doubt as to which group they belonged. To them, freedom meant something fundamentally different from what the slavers and plantation owners meant by it. It meant release from an unconscionable system of human bondage. It meant life, liberty, and the pursuit of happiness. It meant justice.

The road to justice and real freedom would be a long one and, of course, we are not there yet. In many ways, the ongoing pursuit of racial justice and true equality defines the American experience. For many African Americans in the South, it is an essential element of what defines "We."

Backcountry and Cavalier cultures showed clear evidence of inter-dependent, group-oriented cultures, yet they both promoted themselves as champions of a vigorously independent spirit. For slaves, vigorous independence was a desire barely contained inside every breath, and inter-reliance was essential to both physical and psychological survival. How can a fiercely independent people also be collectivists? We turn to eminent Southern sociologist John Shelton Reed for guidance. (Reed's scholarship and insights into the contemporary South are matched only by the pleasure of reading his books.)

THE FIERCELY INDEPENDENT SOUTHERN COLLECTIVIST

It's often been said that the South is a land of contradictions. Perhaps, then, it is no surprise that these contradictions run as deep as Southerners' very concept of identity. Are they fiercely independent individualists or group-minded collectivists?

Sociologist Reed points us toward two types of individualism described by North Carolinian and University of

Chicago philosopher Richard Weaver. The first reflects the absence or rejection of cultural prescriptions and is exemplified in the New Englander Henry David Thoreau. The second is itself culturally prescribed: "One is individualistic because one is supposed to be," Reed writes.[28]

Thoreau's rejection of the norms and conclusions of society place him as a true individualist. He (theoretically) rejected all conclusions of mankind's cultures, only affirming them once he—himself—decided they held merit. For Thoreau, it was clear that individuals should question the tenets of custom and tradition, and that the world should be discovered through our own senses and reasoning. His experiment at Walden Pond wasn't as spartanly independent as some believe (his mother did his laundry while he was there, and he often received guests), but his concept of individualism is truly American.

Perhaps the Southern concept of individualism is best illustrated by its bid for ultimate independence through civil war and by the warrior who would become the most famous military leader of his age. Robert E. Lee "opposed secession, deplored the presence of slavery, and cherished the Union,"* as historian Paul C. Nagel writes in *The Lees of Virginia*.[29] And though he struggled over which army to fight for, in the end, he chose the Confederacy. After turning down the commission to lead the federal army, Lee explained why: "I declined the offer ... saying as candidly and courteously as I could, that though opposed to secession and deprecating war, I could take no part in an invasion of the Southern States."[30]

---

* Lee might have deplored slavery, but he never showed it by freeing his own slaves.

Lee foresaw the wreckage that would come from secession but was compelled to restrain his true independent thought in order to fulfill his sense of duty to his larger group. Of course, this meant he had to resign his commission with the U.S. Army. But it was Virginia that he counted as his homeland of many generations, and it was the collective will of Southern leadership that ultimately commanded his loyalties. Lee knew if he joined the rebellion and lost, the South would pay dearly. Arlington Cemetery—built over his ancestral homeland—stands as witness to what was sacrificed to fulfill his sense of duty to Virginia.

Lee was a fiercely independent Southerner in the sense that he conformed to this Southern ethos, but conformity is not a product of a vigorously individualistic spirit. It is quite the opposite, and he was forced to stifle his own beliefs about civil war in order to become the Southern warrior. Lee was really a duty-bound Southern collectivist, unwilling to separate himself from the group that constituted the "We" to which he belonged.

Any model we use to describe the world suffers from inherent limitations. In creating such models, we must invent the categories that describe physical phenomena or human behavior and then put all our subjects into one box or another. Nuance can be lost or overlooked, and over-categorization can lead to a limited understanding of our subject of study. In this way, any model we use to describe *anything* significantly shapes how we understand the subject.

The more complexity found in our subject, the more resistant it will be to categorical generalizations. The smart people who created these models know this and encourage us to be mindful of the many variations of individuals and cultures. They also know these models offer substantial rewards and can lead to successful, productive interactions. It's for these rewards that over-categorization is risked.

The research that drove early work in this field was focused on resolving differences between very individualistic Western societies and very collectivistic Eastern societies. This was in answer to the many cross-cultural failures experienced between the two hemispheres in the burgeoning international trade of the twentieth century.

In our search for the cultural dynamics of the South, we've seen how Southerners exhibit many qualities of collectivism within the very individualistic United States. While the cultural differences between Poughkeepsie and Pascagoula aren't as great as they are between Chicago and Shanghai, they are still prevalent, creating many of our own cross-cultural mix-ups.

In his excellent book *Individualism and Collectivism*, Triandis offers advice to both cultural types for improving interactions with those from opposite systems.[31] Though Southerners aren't as collectivistic as the Asian cultures he describes, much of his advice is well-suited for newcomers to the South. Culled from Triandis' work and previous chapters in this book, some basic guidance for interacting with other cultural types follows.

SUGGESTIONS FOR INDIVIDUALISTS

Control your ego. Your cultural conditioning drives you toward self-promotion, making you competitive and ambitious. This behavior sets off alarms for Southern collectivists because it poses a threat to group cohesion. Show some restraint in touting your own accomplishments. Southerners value humility and perceive it as a positive personal characteristic.

Develop collaboration skills. Owing to your competitive nature, you expect others to look out for themselves and voice their opinions with the same competitive edge. In your mind, conversation and ideas advance through a sort of challenge and response, with the best ideas winning out. But there can be no victory if there are no other competitors, and you may very well receive hard feelings and exclusion as your reward. Consider and account for the needs of the entire group. Be warm and polite in conversations, as this is the cultural norm.

Learn how to give face. You expect others to herald their own achievements and advocate for themselves. But Southerners value personal humility, preferring to let others speak of their accomplishments. Polite conversational norms in the South are built on other-focused facework that supports the image of others, especially fellow group members. Providing this face support creates good will and helps secure relationships of all types.

Pay attention to context. Because conversations are less direct, individualists should pay closer attention to non-verbal contextual cues. Silence carries meaning in the South, so don't feel you have to fill all the airspace by yourself. Look for meaning in conversational silence, and remember that the collectivist's wheels are still turning, perhaps accounting for unspoken—yet important—contextual factors. You focus on the content of speech in conversation, but much of the meaning for Southerners may be in the context.

Read between the lines. You're a direct speaker and expect the same from others. In the South, indirect speech is often employed as a safe way to present opinions and feelings. Be aware that strong views can hide behind indirect speech, leaving direct speakers clueless as to the intended message. Don't expect Southerners to speak their minds freely and fully. Examine indirect statements for allusions to their real message, and dig deeper if you want the whole story.

Look to group norms to predict opinions and behavior. Southerners can be hard for individualists to read. As indirect speakers who use cultural context to carry meaning, it can be difficult to know where they stand. Since collectivists find identity in their groups, and generally adopt group values and opinions as their own, the norms of their close in-groups are a good indicator of their personal viewpoints.

Discover whether you're perceived as in or out of the group. You will likely be treated better if you're considered a fellow in-group member and worse if you're not. Knowing where you stand can inform how you approach situations: should you be on guard or are you in safe hands? Family or work association doesn't guarantee inclusion into in-groups, but sacrificing for other members does cement membership.

Use smoothing strategies in conflict. You are a direct-speaking and competitive self-promoter who isn't likely to back away from conflict. You're more comfortable with conflict than Southerners are, and you see it as necessary to attain your goals. You're also more willing to forget about discord once the moment passes, but Southerners are not. Casual challenges or small conflicts can carry significant meaning in the South, and perceived slights are not quickly forgotten. Avoid direct criticism that threatens exclusion and learn how to "give face" as a smoothing strategy. By softening criticism and couching it within a context of inclusiveness, you will find a more receptive audience. Abandon direct conflict if the other party can't handle it, and accept that avoidance is a regular conflict strategy for Southerners. Allow time before pursuing the issue again.

Attack face only if you're looking for a fight. We all go looking for a fight sometimes. A great way to start conflict with Southerners is to attack the integrity of their groups or threaten them with exclusion. Expect animosity from the entire group when in conflict with one of its members. If that sounds unpleasant, avoid using direct face attacks.

Understand that heritage and group association are powerful forces. You are not as influenced by your groups or your own heritage. They are important to you, but for Southerners, they are the foundation of identity. As such, they are vigorously maintained and defended, playing major roles in the Southern psyche.

Expect relationships to develop slowly. Relationships are typically developed over a long period of time in the South. Entry into groups requires proper vetting as all members carry some piece of group identity, which is then shared by all members. Because you're used to making and breaking associations as your goals change, you expect relationships to develop quickly. But you're often surprised or hurt when full membership into friend groups is drawn out and delayed. Once you gain entry into Southern circles, expect relationships to carry obligations and duties.

FOR SOUTHERN COLLECTIVISTS

Talk about yourself. You should know that individualists expect you to promote yourself and tout your own achievements. If you don't, they're inclined to think of you as unaccomplished. Individualists prize uniqueness and personal opinions, and they'll be looking for your own unique ideas and opinions too.

Get competitive. Since competition is a norm for individualists, a lack of it suggests a lack of ambition. Understand that competition in individualist systems isn't necessarily an act of ill will. It's simply how things are done. Within these systems, competition determines winners and losers, so if you want to get ahead, you have break through your collaborative tendencies and compete for it.

Accept that autonomy is a high priority for individualists. You know what it's like to need your space, but you have a much higher tolerance to obligations and duties than individualists. They need more autonomy in their personal and work lives than you, and they are put off when others make unwarranted claims on their personal space. They can work well with others and need companionship like everyone else, but at the end of the day, they insist on directing their own lives. Allow them the space to do so.

Focus on the content of conversations. Your indirect speaking style requires that others fully and correctly interpret your intended message. If your audience doesn't communicate this way, your message won't be heard. As Low Context communicators, individualists will expect the specific content of your language to carry all of your meaning. Content is king, and you will be better understood if you deliver your message with fullness and clarity.

Be more direct with your opinions and ideas. Individualists are going to tell you what they think, and they expect the same out of you. They can be forceful advocates for their own ideas and opinions and use competitive conversation to sort out the most preferable option. You tend to find such direct competition unpleasant and may get your feelings hurt when others compete against you. Opposition shouldn't be read as a *personal* rebuke but, rather, as a challenge to your ideas. Individualists will not combine the two if they aren't related. Speak your mind directly and expect no one to take it personally.

Present yourself with consistency. As you move from one social context to another, you're inclined to behave in a way appropriate for each setting. This confuses individualists. You see yourself as expressing the full range of your personality across multiple contexts, but they value consistency in all settings. Their communication norms lead them to fully express themselves in all situations, which you often read as inappropriate. It is the way of the individualist, however, and they are suspicious of inconsistencies in behavior.

Be mindful of your particularism. You tend to look out for your own and expect that others do the same. Your desire to protect and promote fellow group members is strong, but it can violate the individualistic sense of fairness. As universalists, they believe special treatment to fellow in-group members is unfair and perhaps even immoral. Don't expect individualists to break the rules in order to accommodate fellow group members.

Don't take it personally when conflict is handled directly. You prefer to handle conflict indirectly and will avoid it altogether if the potential harm to relationships is too great. But individualists don't mix the issues with the people involved, so conflict is limited to the issue at hand. With the danger to relationships out of the way, individualists are able to use conflict to forge solutions and agreements.

Argue objectively. In individualistic systems, persuasive arguments based on subjective factors will lose out to objective arguments that meet stated goals. You are group minded and approach problems with collaborative solutions. You want to account for subjective factors, especially how others are affected. In your mind, subjective considerations are often understood as important to attaining objective solutions. They may be, but individualists are more likely to be convinced by objective arguments.

Expect to be judged on your own merits. Your group associations are of little meaning to individualists who will evaluate you based on your own qualities. Individualists see each person as self-construed and self-contained. Since they use less cultural context than you, they depend upon self-expressions as evidence of character. You are the source of those self-expressions.

Accept that relationships are often transient. You're still pretty close to your besties from middle school. You have long-lived relationships and family connections that you expect to last a lifetime. Individualists will open up quickly and share their lives with you, but they also tend to move on quickly and leave friendships behind. As their goals and interests shift, their friendships and relational circles shift too. Accept that individualists don't view personal sacrifice as necessary to the maintenance of relational circles. They often will sacrifice for others, but they don't see it as an obligation.

The individualism-collectivism model is used internationally to facilitate cross-cultural relationships in business, politics, science, and many other areas where we come together. It's also a useful way to understand the cultural differences witnessed between Southerners and other Americans. While useful, it is not perfect. Some people will strongly represent the qualities of their culture and some will not.

We all have individualistic *and* collectivistic aspects to our psychological composition, but we have them at different mixtures.[32] If you're from the Northeast, you likely have a stronger mix of individualism. If you're from the South, you likely have a stronger mix of collectivism. And while many other factors contribute to a person's nature—personality, generation, gender, socio-economic background, and many more—a working understanding of individualistic and collectivistic cultures can greatly improve the effectiveness of our cross-cultural interactions.

When we're able to recognize the tendencies of collectivism or individualism within ourselves, we're able to understand ourselves better and improve how we communicate with others even in our own culture. Are we being too direct for this environment, or too indirect? Will competitive conversation be perceived as an offense, or will it enhance our prospects?

By recognizing the dominant cultural norms surrounding us, we can see how our own tendencies are favored or not, and thereby make adjustments to how we converse and interact with others. Awareness of both the cultural environment *and* our personal style empowers us to more effectively communicate with all people, playing to our strengths and minimizing our weaknesses.

CHAPTER SEVEN

Working Down South

Collectivists enter the workplace with different priorities, goals, and expectations than do individualists. While no surprise to international business managers, these psychological dynamics are generally unrecognized by the rest of us, especially within our own countries. Our common American culture often blinds us to the contrasting perspectives found in our nation, creating work environments that unintentionally undermine the potential of individuals and organizations alike.

The premise of this book is that Southern culture shows collectivistic qualities in a very individualistic country, and that if we understand the predominant qualities of both, we can better communicate and more successfully interact with each other. Along the way, we've seen that individuals in any culture can exhibit behavior contrary to their cultural archetype. So even in a very individualistic culture like that found in the northeastern U.S., a substantial percentage of people exhibit collectivistic qualities, or at least do so at a level greater than their cultural norm. The same is true in the collectivistic South—some people run counter to the dominant cultural norms. We've also seen that people everywhere will display characteristics of both individualism and collectivism at different times. These behaviors are ubiquitous in our lives but tricky to categorize.

However, awareness of our own culture's *predominant* tendencies, and that of others, can lead to a more empathetic and competent approach to life. In the workplace, this translates to an empowered workforce that can better communicate with all cultural types and better serve the needs of clients, coworkers, and the company as a whole.

We-oriented collectivists are more likely to value sociability at work,[1] and they show it by seeking relationships and interconnectedness in work settings. Group-focused and innately aware of relational dynamics, the Southern collectivist tends to search for and find group association within the workplace. Those attentive to the needs of the group are rewarded in these environments.

I-oriented individualists are concerned with establishing personal esteem and value within a company. Self-focused and ambitious, the archetypical individualist prioritizes autonomy, advancement, recognition, and earnings in their working lives.[2] In theory, the most able and effective individuals are rewarded in the workplace.

These two cultural styles prove difficult to reconcile in their purest forms, on the far ends of the spectrum. One cultural type brings a collaborative approach to the workplace, while the other thrives under the stress of competition.

Most of us have worked with extreme versions of these cultural types, though our own position on the spectrum may affect how "extreme" we find the behavior to be.

Competitive individualists, with their own norms and standards, first seek success and rewards for themselves. Perhaps an extreme version of this inspired the mantra "greed is good" in the film *Wall Street*. Many actual Wall Streeters openly embrace this attitude as well, though they would likely reference Adam Smith's *The Wealth of Nations* and his "invisible hand" of free markets to present their argument.

Collaborative collectivists, with *their* own cultural style and standards, first seek group cohesion and harmony, expecting the success of the group or company to also bring social and material security for themselves.[3] Extreme representations are perhaps best found in smaller agrarian economies where the success of the family farm—or of larger groups like clans and communities—is every group member's success.

Most individualists aren't as extreme as the fictional characters in *Wall Street* and can't be understood as embodying the idea that "greed is good." Nor are most modern collectivists properly understood as cooperative farmers working together in clan-based social systems. Moreover, these extremes don't represent the working lives of most Americans. Most of us work and live by standards that are found somewhere closer to the middle of the spectrum, representing a healthier mix of these personal characteristics.

Both outlooks are valid (culture makes it so), but they present quite different approaches to a working life. Their contrasting priorities and goals result in workplaces with fundamentally different rules and norms. They even affect how we judge whether a job is done well or not.

Ability and effort are qualities both cultural types use to evaluate performance in the workplace. However, they're often defined in different ways. Triandis points us toward a formula used to illustrate how we determine performance in individualistic systems: Ability × Effort = Performance.[4] The more ability one has, and the more effort put behind it, the higher and better the performance will be. This is true for both cultural types, but notice in this formula that the two qualities are conceived as having a multiplying effect on each other. So a very good mechanic, software designer, or brain surgeon who expends great effort should have an exponentially higher overall performance than their equally skilled counterparts who expend less. Those who work hard at their occupation but start with less ability will also come up short in this formula. The idea here is that each input—ability and effort—is independent of the other and deficiencies in one category can't be fully remedied by strengths in the other.

A purely collectivistic approach to measuring performance uses a slightly different formulation. For them, Ability + Effort = Performance.[5] This formula is conceived as a summation rather than a multiplication of the two variables, *equalizing* the importance of each input. Being group-oriented, the collectivist is driven to account for all members of an in-group. So if one person has less ability, the deficit can be overcome by expending more effort. Someone else in the group who brings a lot of ability (skill, knowledge, capital, etc.) may feel it is up to others to match this with a high level of effort. In this way, it becomes a fair exchange for group members while maintaining group co-hesiveness and harmony. It is, perhaps, not so obvious in the modern South, but this dynamic is still in play, if to a lesser degree.

The business of hiring, promoting, and firing are all affected by one's cultural outlook. Collectivists will often hire fellow in-group members over others outside of their groups, even if the others are more qualified.[6] Skills and abilities are certainly important, but promotions are gener-ally based on loyalty and seniority, which strengthens group bonds and inspires loyalty from members.[7] Firing isn't al-ways based on poor performance—collectivists prefer to reassign the less able to more suitable tasks, maintaining the cohesion of the in-group.[8] Falling out of favor with the in-group is a more likely reason for dismissal.

Individualists tend to examine one's personal attributes when hiring, firing, and promoting in the workplace. Tal-ents and abilities (including interpersonal skills) are the most important factors when making these decisions.[9] This promotes a competitive—and theoretically meritocratic—system where the most qualified are hired and promoted. Individualists perceive the workplace as the embodiment of a contract between the employer and employee,[10] and failure from either side to fulfill that agreement provides reason to break the contract.

Both systems are liable to hire or promote the wrong people. The collectivist risks hiring and promoting a less able (though more senior and loyal) person. And the winning attributes that satisfy individualist sensibilities—self-confidence, competitiveness, and autonomy—don't necessarily match the skills associated with strong leadership and management of others.

The differences in what we're motivated to achieve in the workplace, who we hire, and how we evaluate performance are fundamental to our approach to work and what we expect in return from it. If we recognize these different perspectives as legitimate (instead of backward or dangerously selfish), we gain some advantages both for ourselves and our business. Validating the different perspectives of others is the first step toward meeting their needs and expectations—whether they are clients, colleagues, or all the people in the department following your lead.

Southerners perceive direct, competitive speech as offensive and threatening. They often respond with indirect and ambiguous speech, confounding Low Context speakers. Motivations on both sides are misunderstood, and this often results in inter-office dysfunction.

The workplace is perceived as a competitive environment in individualistic systems, making conversation and self-presentation competitive as well. In an individualist's perfect world, the best ideas and most talented people win the day. Direct and confident assertions are expected to be met with competitive retorts and direct challenges. If this doesn't happen, they are left without feedback to discover the best way forward.

Bringing this mindset into the Southern workplace is risky, and an offender can be quickly judged as an out-group member. This is a precarious situation in collectivistic workplaces and is best avoided. The stakes are raised when individualists are charged with leading collectivists.

Leading and managing collectivistic Southerners involves the soft skills of relationship building, High Context communication, and collaborative facework. Southerners' We-focused outlook motivates them to find security through group association in their personal lives and at work. Disrupting these group associations or violating their need for security is likely to create hard feelings.

Consider this hypothetical example:

A struggling small business in the South is sold and, after the consultants finish their work, the new owners bring in a fresh management team to turn things around. The incoming general manager—who has an individualist's outlook and we'll call Monty—is friendly and excited enough to leave a favorable first impression on the staff.

Unfortunately for Monty (as well as the staff and new owners), the problems begin with his second impression. This is at the company-wide meeting where he introduces the new leadership's vision for the future. The company's dozen employees gather to hear this vision with some trepidation, which could be expected anywhere. More of a challenge for Monty is that his actual vision for company operations is never really heard. His speech so thoroughly violates their collectivist-oriented needs that it leaves them with only one message: there is danger and trouble ahead.

Monty confidently begins by presenting his credentials and qualifications to lead the company. He is firm and insistent about these, never wavering in his self-assurance. This part of the speech reaches its culmination with the line "I am extremely good at what I do." Monty scans the room to make eye contact with everyone while he matter-of-factly repeats this. The team finds this more than a little braggadocious and becomes suspicious of both Monty's character and the veracity of his claims.

The employees have plenty at stake in the company's future and are the only ones in the room who were there for its past. Monty meets this reality with a wall of self-promotion, presenting himself as brimming with energy and know-how. They will have the opportunity to learn from the best, he says, and everything about him exudes the message: "I am supremely talented and will run circles around our competitors and everyone else." The staff, gathered in a circle around him, heard this message as: "I am a supremely self-centered asshole and will be the proverbial bull in your china shop." They fear the worst. Monty immediately delivers.

Figuring all transitions involve staff changes, he decides to get ahead of the curve. "Only the *best* will work with me at this company." Monty loved this part of his speech. "That's just the way it is with me: the best or nothing. Buy into what I'm doing here and you will join the best—you will become the best. Don't buy into it and, well, I have twenty-five people right now who would love to come here and work for me." This was a strategic move on Monty's part: he was motivating his staff and putting a competitive fire in their bellies. Unfortunately, the staff heard something like this: "I have no interest in your security and no respect for the integrity of this group."

Monty didn't stay with the company very long. He did shake up the staff, but he under-delivered in most every category. He had oversold his talents and received little help from the disgruntled employees who felt Monty wasn't part of their "We." In the end, his leadership was an unqualified failure.

Monty's intention was to present the new vision for the company and inspire the staff to get on board. But that's not what got through to the staff. Their takeaway from the big meeting was all about the *real* dangers Monty posed to group security, cohesiveness, and harmony. These were received as active threats to their highest priorities.

Monty wanted to establish his credentials and exhibit his unstoppable, goal-focused drive. This was meant as a positive, pro-social message that would display his worthy qualities as their new leader. From his perspective, ability and effort are the pathway to high performance, and he wanted to announce with confidence that he had both. He was right to attempt building credibility and trust with the staff, but his natural approach came off as self-aggrandizing and produced the opposite feeling—distrust. Because relationships are long-developed and because in-group boundaries are relatively fixed, Monty's self-exhortations won him no credibility and no buy-in. His actions could only be understood as those of an unsubstantiated braggart.

Hofstede advises individualists working in collectivist systems to focus on relationships, as they are often prioritized over the tasks at hand.[11] New relationships rely on the cultural norms of pleasant and polite interactions. More developed relationships may require obligations and duties, cementing mutual interconnection. By establishing relationships first, the task-minded individualist has paved the way to achieving their own goals.

Monty could have easily broadened his leadership style to satisfy collectivistic priorities without compromising his individualistic goals. Had he respected the priorities and needs found in the Southern workplace, the door would have been open for him to *prove* he had the skills for the job. And had he received buy-in from the staff, their sense of loyalty would likely have driven them to extraordinary lengths to serve the larger needs of the group. But instead, he marked himself as a threat, and the staff judged him to be an outsider. From there, he was already doomed to failure.

Competitive communication risks drowning out quieter voices and can leave conversations without important points of view. The best idea in the room may be left unheard if its speaker doesn't join the competition. Worse, talented employees may leave the company if their input isn't being sought and their needs aren't being addressed. Low Contexters working in the South would do well to listen for those quieter, more indirect voices.

There are many possible strategies that can lead to improved communication between individualists and collectivists in the workplace. Because every person brings their own specific qualities, needs, and preferences to any situation, there are no satisfying one-size-fits-all answers. Rather, awareness of our personal style allows us to tailor a successful approach anywhere. Consider the strategy employed in this hypothetical situation at a university down south:

Dr. Larson knows who he is. He should. As a 65-year-old itinerant scholar, he's lived the life of a traveling researcher and professor, following the money needed to continue his impressive research around the country. He's met many types of people along the way and almost all of them let him know at one point or another that he is a difficult and different kind of person. Not a bad person. Actually, he is a really good person by most people's standards. But his style is often interpreted as aggressive and combative instead of passionate and driven, which is really closer to the mark. He *is* friendly and supportive, but this is usually driven at warp speed and comes with a competitive edge. That is his method. And the truth is his ever-present goal.

He knows who he is, and he has good evidence to support his conclusions. Now that he's getting older and has made a name for himself in the field, he is careful to properly introduce his style to new colleagues. Experience has taught him to be especially careful in two situations: with younger people who won't challenge him because of his authority, or with Southerners who outright won't accept him because of his style. The latter he learned the hard way.

He knows he can send signals he doesn't intend. So over time he developed an exercise to introduce himself and his style to new colleagues. This was especially important as his career advanced and he was leading large research teams.

When Dr. Larson receives an offer from a Southern university, it's one he can't refuse. It is an ideal situation for his research. Excited to get started and meet his new team, he dusts off his Meet-the-Weirdo presentation and prepares to introduce himself. His team arrives, exchanging pleasantries over coffee, and Dr. Larson asks them to have a seat for a short exercise.

"I want to tell you about how I like to work and think and live," he said, smiling and warming up the crowd. He already shows signs of his manic energy. "Actually, I probably *need* to tell you this, because I've been told I can be difficult and argumentative. But! Argumentation is my way to get at the thing we're after—better answers, better ideas, and better work. I like my work to be challenged, and I need you guys to provide those challenges. Don't be shy. I will challenge *your* ideas and work, and I do this in the spirit of finding those better answers." Dr. Larson paces and hops around the room with his hands and arms flying in a secret and strange sort of sign language.

"A colleague of mine once told me that I approach science as if it was a full-contact sport. That was several decades ago, and I'm much changed—better, my wife would say. But that made me realize that my style was standing in the way of the work and everyone's happiness.

"So, I developed this little presentation." He clicks a button and a picture of a miserable looking cat in a cowboy outfit popped onto the projection screen. The team laughs. "So what do you think when you see this?" The group quietly smiles and chuckles, not quite sure what to think of the cowboy cat or the man presenting it. No one is willing to venture a response until, finally, someone mumbles out, "It's cute."

"Okay, I disagree," he replies matter-of-factly. "That is not a picture of cuteness. That is a picture of a cat being tortured by its owners." He pauses. "But then again, I have to question my own analysis. It's possible the cat is getting ready for an alley showdown, and its 'miserable' face is really its 'tough' face. If its little guns are real, I'd bet on the showdown and that, I admit, would be downright cute. But if they're fake, I'm not so sure." He says all of this and more in a few seconds, racing through his thoughts. No one offers a rebuttal.

"Wait. Look closer at the cowboy outfit. Does anyone see a clue in this?"

One of them raises his hand: "It's blue and silver, and his hat looks like it possibly has a Dallas Cowboys star on the side of it."

"Bingo! We've found a clue that diminishes my two previous ideas. With this, we probably know much more about the cat and its parents. Everyone agrees that Cowboys fans are immoral and unpleasant, so the cat is probably upset at its parentage *and* outfit." He could get away with this because he wasn't in Texas. And he gets away with it for some time, badmouthing the Cowboys fan base in his argumentative and acerbic style. "Now, does anyone disagree with that?"

Again, the team didn't know what to think or say.

"Is anyone here a Cowboys fan?" Sheepishly, one of them raises his hand, prompting Dr. Larson to let out a victorious "Yes!" He goes on to bait the younger man into a ridiculous, lighthearted argument. Dr. Larson argues every immoral-Cowboys angle with passion and a combative edge, goading the Cowboys fan into counter-argument. Finally, Dr. Larson is made to concede the undeniable: Cowboys fandom doesn't necessarily indicate immorality. He was wrong and had been proven to be so. He admits as much and thanks the Cowboys fan for showing him the truth.

"Okay, I hope this was fun. I just want to let you see my communication style with something that doesn't matter. Next time, we'll argue whether Cowboys fandom is a *precursor* to immorality." The team laughs. "No, no. We're done with that. We'll have many serious subjects to discuss—or argue about—and I need you to know that when I'm like that—which is pretty much all the time—it's nothing to do with you on a personal level. When I challenge your work or you challenge mine, it's the work we're being 'aggressive' toward."

He has one last point to get across in this introductory meeting, which he believes is especially important for a team of Southerners.

"Lastly, let me say that my door is always open—well, almost always. We all have lives to attend to outside of work. And for me, there are a lot of meetings that come with the job. But, I want you to know that you can bring anything to me for discussion. This is a team project, after all.

"However, I also want you to take risks and be willing to venture out on your own." Dr. Larson became quieter and more serious. "The best research happens when we take those risks and get outside of our comfort zone. We'll be wrong a lot, but if we're right once, we win.

"Don't just look to me for answers because I won't necessarily have them. You'll be in the driver's seat with the work in front of you. Apply your own knowledge and intuition, and take those independent risks. I'll have your back."

Based on his experience working in the South, Dr. Larson knows that some researchers here are less inclined to take initiative. Collectivists tend to seek approval for every move and would like to have those with more experience show them the way. This is sometimes called "handholding," and it is common in collectivistic systems. Dr. Larson has chosen to accommodate the handholding impulse, but he also encourages them to take independent risks.

Dr. Larson is self-aware of how others perceive him and wants to get out in front of the potential problem. He hopes to set up a happy, productive work environment and knows that his oft-acerbic style can stand in the way of that. By inoculating his staff to his manner, they will better know how to take him. He is a direct, Low Context speaker, and there's no changing that. His cross-cultural strategy is as straightforward as his style: embrace who he is, warn everyone, and try to improve on his personal challenges.

Most everyone would like high-paying, personally fulfilling work in which their abilities are valued and their workplace relationships are satisfying. But we often have to make trade-offs in these areas, receiving less of one in exchange for more of another. Hopefully, our trade-offs are well matched to our priorities and we're fortunate enough to score a position that satisfies our most important needs.

Recognizing our various needs and priorities in the workplace gives us the opportunity to address them as legitimate and important. Using the language and concepts of the individualism-collectivism model, we're better able to understand ourselves and others. This enables us to better balance everyone's needs and forge a happy work life.

Too often, personal conflict and miscommunication hinder the productivity of a company and the happiness of its employees. But if cultural differences are seen as opportunities to harness the strengths of each perspective while mitigating weaknesses, higher productivity and more harmonious workplaces can be created.

The cliché "successful businesses are built on relationships" is even more true in the American South than elsewhere in our country. While in the South, your prospects will be much improved if you develop and pay attention to relationships at every level of your organization.

CHAPTER EIGHT

Adapting to the Newest South

There is no "unifying theory" from the social sciences that can describe to satisfaction the bewilderingly varied behavior of humans and the societies we develop. There are too many variables within us—personality, gender, age, generation, economic background, the kind of day we're having, et cetera—for any cultural model to encompass every individual (or individual action) and flawlessly predict or fully explain human behavior.

Cultures and societies, too, are composed of many variables that shape the specific behaviors and characteristics of the people within them. We are all a mix of different variables at different ratios at different times. We are complex, and our motivations and behaviors reflect this.

Luckily for us, our minds are well prepared to deal with this complexity *if*—and this is essential—*if* we don't limit our understanding of the world to our own system of norms, beliefs, and customs. By expanding our awareness of other systems, we gain the ability to view reality through other prisms and better understand the behavior of other people. Seeing things from another perspective expands our own understanding of what it means to be alive which, in turn, enables us to seek a more full and rewarding life. Put another way (and without apology for repetition of the sentiment): if we free our minds, our asses will follow.

The contrasts found between cultures are the delight of seasoned travelers. It's there, in the friction of differing approaches to the universal human situation, that the mysteries of life reveal themselves. Through our differences, we're presented with the unique and paradoxical opportunity to identify *our similarities*, which are too often hidden in the blind spots of our own cultural conditioning. And it's through the recognition of our similarities that cultural differences are made secondary to the common need to make this whole thing work out.

The ideas presented in this book are meant to guide the reader toward an awareness of *predominant* cultural tendencies and the motivations that drive them. But these tendencies are only that—tendencies—and their expression will be shaped by a complex and changing ratio of variables within each person. It would be risky to use these ideas as if they were a diagnostic tool kit, where "x" behavior should be met with "y" reaction. It would also be no fun.

The broad categories that are described as individualistic and collectivistic are fundamentally different starting points from which we engage the world. Awareness of these differences offers us a new way to understand and value others. It also presents the opportunity to better understand life and develop ourselves as more capable to meet its challenges.

And the challenges are many—not just in the American South but across the country and in every corner of the world. Everywhere across the globe we face the many issues related to having seven billion people inhabiting our little planet. Our ability to transcend cultural boundaries and solve our common challenges will determine what our shared future looks like. Perhaps it begins by simply recognizing that other norms, beliefs, and customs are just as valid and important to other cultures as our own is to us.

INDIVIDUALISM AND COLLECTIVISM AROUND THE WORLD

Most of the world's cultures are considered to be on the collectivistic side of the individualism-collectivism spectrum. In early human societies, collectivism is assumed as the baseline cultural approach, one that was required to survive an untamed world. Though modern cultures are very different from pre-historic ones in many ways, the basic need for survival and interconnection hasn't changed, allowing this cultural perspective to endure as the dominant cultural type. Individualistic cultures are in the minority, and they are associated with a few precursor conditions.[1]

Ethnic diversity, wealth, and a fast rate of social change are all *possible* factors that can lead cultures to become more individualistic. It's easy to see how these factors are interrelated, for instance, in historic capitals of trade and commerce. Commercial cities are centers of wealth and meeting places of the world's cultures. Both factors accelerate the rate of change in society.

Collectivistic cultures tend to be more ethnically homogenous, resulting in a common cultural background with belief systems that are largely unchallenged by outside influences.[2] Members of these systems are group-oriented and driven to protect traditional values.

Individualistic cultures tend to have more diverse points of view among their people, with ideas from many different mother cultures in the pot.[3] In these more diverse systems, there is no shared, long-developed cultural background that holds sway as one undeniable force. Individuals can explore other ideas and conceive the world for themselves. A self-directed archetype develops out of this environment, creating a self-identity that is internally based. As new cultures develop from the combining of many others, the sway of traditional cultures over individuals is lessened.

Greater wealth in societies is strongly correlated with individualism. In wealthier economies, members have more ability to choose their own direction and establish an identity outside the boundaries of traditional group norms and beliefs. People in poorer societies have fewer opportunities to step outside cultural boundaries and less motivation to distinguish themselves from the group.[4] Interdependence plays a key social role in less economically advanced cultures, driving collectivistic value systems.

An accelerated rate of social change may also push cultures toward the individualistic side of the spectrum. Technological advances, economic development, immigration, and changing social values can alter or eliminate established cultural meanings.[5] When this happens quickly, any shared system of beliefs, customs, and communication must expand to include (or, at least, account for) the social change. As traditional ideas become less relevant in modern contexts, individuals find new ways to understand the world and new definitions of themselves within it.

But human cultures are too complex to easily fall into tidy categories, and these possible precursors for individualism only tell part of the story. As Hofstede points out in *Cultures and Organizations*, Japanese culture has felt the embrace of modernity and yet strongly retains many collectivistic characteristics.[6] Of course, no one knows how this plays out over time. Japan had been insular for many centuries and only relatively recently became the more open and international economic powerhouse that it is today. However, it is difficult to imagine the Japanese culture and character changing too much, too quickly.

The same might be true for Southern culture, whose members seem strongly motivated to retain some form of traditional culture. The cultural impulse to retain traditional values must also be accompanied by the historical opportunity to do so. For Japan, perhaps it is made possible by the long isolation and homogeneity of its culture, despite its modernity. For the South, perhaps the historical opportunity to retain a collectivistic system involves its historical isolation and relative poverty.

In the seventeenth-century Cavalier South, we see a concept of Virginia as the embodiment of a perfect rank-and-class society that need never change. This isolating cultural outlook was matched by an isolated settlement pattern. The backcountry Scotch-Irish were also geographically isolated and profoundly connected to their way of life and collectivistic system. In the Deep South, we see a land that was hastily transformed into another iteration of a seventeenth-century plantation economy, one that was just as quickly undermined by the failure of its doomed precepts.

Secession and civil war would bind these collectivist subcultures into one political and historical concept that we call the South. The social collapse that followed the Civil War would keep its economy less developed and its people isolated until well into the twentieth century.

As the modern South continues to develop and change, the traditional qualities of its culture will continue to be challenged. Time will show how societal developments affect the collectivistic outlook of Southerners, but as with Japan, it's hard to imagine the South losing its cultural perspective anytime soon.

The degree of individualism or collectivism changes in both cultures and people over time. Globalization and technology are driving social change faster than ever, perhaps pushing all collectivistic cultures toward the individualist side of the spectrum and even driving individualists to reconsider the costs of unbridled personal ambition.

The historically collectivistic cultures of China and Japan are undeniably becoming more individualistic with each generation as social changes create environments that foster a more self-focused perspective. Yet the Chinese and Japanese cultures still strongly exhibit collectivistic traits. Highly individualistic cultures like the U.S. and England seem to be finding the limits and costs of raw individualistic ambition to people, societies, and economies.

Perhaps this is why the American South has captured anew the curiosity of people from around the country and world. Southern culture, in its many manifestations, offers the promise of belonging, of being connected to others through community and tradition. Some see a promise of connection to the land or nature or music or a more "real" lifestyle. Some might just see better weather and lower tax rates.

Whatever the case, newcomers to the present-day South should expect to adapt themselves to the Southern culture they find—it's not likely to change overnight.

THE SOUTH *Is* RISING AGAIN

Southern economies and populations are undoubtedly on the rise. The question is what kind of South will be elevated alongside its fortunes. What societal values and goals do we want to be the hallmarks of the Newest South? What will it look like in terms of economy, politics, and civic culture?

All Americans are bound together by a larger destiny. All Americans have a relevant stake in the future of the South. Those who consider this region as less impactful to our country's future should take a closer look at what the South is and what it's becoming.

As was mentioned in Chapter One, the regions of the South, Midwest, and Northeast had roughly equal populations in the 1950s. This period saw the economic boom of the postwar years open up the South, bringing interstates, industry, and opportunities where little had been before. Sixty years later, the population of this region stands on the brink of overtaking both the Midwest and Northeast combined. And the largest regional GDP, by far, is found in the South.

This region had a mostly impoverished, agrarian-based economy from the Reconstruction period through World War II. Unsurprisingly, this motivated many Southerners to leave for better opportunities in other parts of the country. In the first half of the twentieth century, Southerners of all backgrounds hitched their fortunes to stars in the Northeast, Midwest, and the still very young Western states, resulting in a population outflow from the South for many decades. In the 1950s, a better economic landscape and a "New South" began to lure white Americans back to this region. This wasn't the case yet for black Americans. The denial of their civil rights would continue to make the South a dangerous place short on opportunity.[7]

African Americans fled the institutionalized racial oppression of the Southern states for better lives elsewhere. Most settled in northern cities where industry was booming and civil rights protections were much greater. This "Great Migration" of black Americans out of the South would begin to turn around as these cities deindustrialized in the 1970s. Job markets collapsed in cities like New York, Chicago and Los Angeles, motivating African Americans to head back to the South as opportunities grew and civil rights protections expanded.[8]

A striking story is told by the 1910, 1970, and 2010 U.S. Censuses regarding populations of African Americans. The three states with the largest black populations in 1910 were Georgia, Mississippi, and Alabama—90% lived in Southern states. In 1970, they were New York, Illinois and California, and only 53% of black Americans lived in the South. The 2010 census showed New York, Florida, and Texas topping the list with roughly equal black populations. Today, black Southerners make up 57% of the total population of African Americans, and that number is growing, accounting for 20% of the overall population of Southern states.[9]

Since the 1990s, the South has seen more African Americans move into the region from all other U.S. regions than have moved out. "Most of the major Great Migration destination states—such as New York, Illinois, Michigan, and California—are now among the greatest contributors to the new southern migration gains," William H. Frey writes in *Diversity Explosion*.[10] This reversal seems to indicate that both civil rights protections and economic opportunities have continued to improve for blacks in the South, at least in certain places.

The Hispanic population is growing quickly in some parts of the South and not much at all in others.[11] Hispanics from many different countries and cultures are drawn to the South for the same reasons all immigrants are drawn to growing economies: opportunities to work, gain education, and generally improve their lives. (Generations of Southerners who left their homeland were motivated by the same goals.) The many mother cultures of Hispanic populations shouldn't be understood as producing just one archetypical "Hispanic." There are significant differences between the various cultures of our friends further south. And, of course, many Hispanics are U.S. citizens, some for many generations.

However, a significant cultural feature is shared amongst almost all the cultures of Central and South America, as well as Mexico: collectivistic cultural traits. Family, religion, duty, and honor are major forces for the people of these cultures, who are strongly influenced by their cultural traditions. Hispanics and Southerners may have different backgrounds (though maybe not), but they share a fundamental approach to the world: "We are."

The South is obviously much more diverse than is presented here, and it will continue to become so alongside the rest of the country and world. Given that race-based slavery was legal in this region only 150 years ago, perhaps it is of greater importance to Southerners that we ensure human rights and opportunity for all people. Given the history of racial violence and discrimination all across our country, perhaps the South can use this period of growth and change to become a positive paradigm of racial and cultural harmony. The opportunities are many.

As the future unfolds, there is a newer South rising. One whose destiny is not yet determined. Modern Southerners of all backgrounds and origins are charged with meeting this destiny with open minds and hearts, rising to meet the challenges—both old and new—that duty asks of them. Perhaps the self-sacrificing, group-focused Southern collectivist will prove to be a strong force in our continuing march forward.

And perhaps all Southerners will ask themselves again: Who are "We?"

How large will that circle of inclusiveness be in the newest South?

ADAPTING, NOT ADOPTING

Ignorance, laziness, or fear of the unknown are common states from which we stereotype other cultures and other people. But stereotypes, and the misguided assumptions that accompany them, can also come from a place of knowledge, especially a little knowledge.

When we're sure we understand something, we look for and find proof that supports that understanding, often ignoring contradictory evidence. If we stop our exploration there, leaving our abilities of perception and critical thinking unutilized, we lose the opportunity to know our subject more fully. This is known as *confirmation bias*. It's an enemy of critical thinking and seemingly endemic to the human race. The cycle of stereotyping and confirmation bias creates a gap between reality and how that reality is understood. When we depend on it to explain our world, we are not doing the harder—but more rewarding—work of honestly engaging life.

We should be careful our cross-cultural efforts don't bleed into assumptions and stereotypes, especially if we haven't lived in or come to know a culture through meaningful experience. We should also be careful and search many sources to inform our understanding of other cultures, not relying on just a few experiences or one little guidebook (for example, this little guidebook).

What we've learned regarding the High Context, collectivistic Southerner as contrasted against the Low Context, individualistic American character provides a basis to begin our understanding of cross-cultural problems everywhere. However, without an open and engaged mind, our knowledge and abilities aren't worth much.

Living or traveling through other cultures doesn't require us to relinquish our own values or preferences. Nor should we delegitimize our own needs or worldview. However, we are better able to serve our values and outlook if we can better communicate them to others, and that means we must adapt to our new environments. We need not adopt other values, but we must defer to the communication norms of our audiences. In no way does this diminish our position—it strengthens it.

The South is undoubtedly in the midst of a larger cultural transformation as economic opportunities continue to improve and a diversity of perspectives continue to flourish within it. Southern culture, like all cultures, must adapt and change to accommodate new voices and new ideas. Time will show us how these transformations unfold and what they mean to the region and our country.

In the meantime, if we hope to work and live well together, we must begin by validating the perspectives of others, finding our various American dreams through a shared existence. We are all Americans with common values, challenges, and goals.

And we are all responsible for the present and future of our *United* States.

Notes

Chapter One

[1.] Michel de Montaigne, *The Complete Works of Michel de Montaigne*, ed. William Hazlitt (New York: J.J. Little and Company, 1988), 136, accessed through Google Books August 4, 2015, https://books.google.com/books?id=yvA5AQAAIAAJ&printsec=frontcover&dq=-complete+works+of+michael+montaigne&hl=en&sa=X-&ved=0CCgQ6AEwAGoVChMIt8b2m8Gwy-AIVylw-Ch2Vzwuj#v=onepage&q=complete%20works%20of%20michael%20montaigne&f=false.

[2.] Richard D. Lewis, *When Cultures Collide* (Boston: Nicholas Brealey International, 2006), 17.

[3.] "The Process of Cultural Conditioning," in *Culture Matters*, Peace Corps International, accessed August 4, 2015 http://files.peacecorps.gov/wws/interactive/culturematters/ch1/culturalconditioning.html.

4. Raven Molloy, Christopher L. Smith, and Abigail Wozniak, "Internal Migration in the United States," *Journal of Economic Perspectives* 25, no. 3 (2011): 185, accessed August 4, 2015, http://papers.ssrn.com/sol3/papers.cfm?abstract_id=1956677##.

5. U.S. Census Bureau, "United States Population Growth by Region," accessed August 4, 2015, https://www.census.gov/popclock/data_tables.php?component=growth.

6. U.S. Bureau of Economic Analysis, "Gross Domestic Product by State," accessed August 4, 2015, http://www.bea.gov/itable/iTable.cfm?ReqID=70&step=1–reqid=70&step=10&isuri=1&7007=2014&7036=-1&7003=900&7035=-1&7006=91000,92000,93000,94000,95000,96000,97000,98000&7001=1900&7002=1&7090=70&7004=naics&7005=-1&7093=levels.

Chapter Two

1. Bertram Wyatt-Brown, "C. Vann Woodward (1908–99)," *Perspectives on History*, March 2000, accessed August 4, 2015, http://www.historians.org/publications-and-directories/perspectives-on-history/march-2000/in-memoriam-c-vann-woodward.

2. C. Vann Woodward, "The Search for Southern Identity," in *The Burden of Southern History* (Baton Rouge: Louisiana State University Press, 1960, 1982 enlarged ed.), 16–25.

3. Ibid., 16.

4. Ibid., 17–18.

5. Ibid., 18.

6. Ibid., 19.

7. Ibid., 19–20.

8. Ibid., 20.

9. Ibid., 21.

10. Ibid., 22–23.

11. Thornton Wilder, "Toward an American Language," in *Thornton Wilder: American Characteristics and Other Essays*, ed. Donald Gallup (New York: Harper and Row, 1979), 16–17.

12. Woodward, 24; Wilder, 44.

13. C. Vann Woodward, "The Historical Dimension," in *The Burden of Southern History* (1960; Baton Rouge: Louisiana State University Press, 1982 enlarged ed.), 27–39.

14. Ibid., 30.

15. Ibid., 31.

16. Ibid., 37.

17. Thomas Wolfe, *You Can't Go Home Again* (1934) (New York: Harper and Row, 1998), 36.

18. Fred Hobson, ed., *William Faulkner's Absalom, Absalom!: A Casebook* (New York: Oxford University Press, 2003), 287.

19. Ralph Waldo Emerson, *Self-Reliance* (1841; *Ralph Waldo Emerson Texts*, 2001), accessed Aug. 4, 2015, http://www.emersoncentral.com/selfreliance.htm.

20. David Hackett Fischer, *Albion's Seed: Four British Folkways in America,* (New York: Oxford University Press, 1989), 33.

21. Morris Talpalar, *The Sociology of Colonial Virginia,* (New York: Philosophical Library, 1960), 52.

22. Kevin Phillips, *The Cousins' Wars: Religion, Politics, and the Triumph of Anglo-America,* (New York: Basic Books, 1999), 24.

23. Fischer, 210.

24. Ibid., 244–245.

25. Ibid., 241.

26. Ibid., 181–183.

27. Ibid., 390.

28. Talpalar, 129.

29. Fischer, 393.

30. Ibid., 155.

31. Ibid., 30.

32. Ibid., 174.

33. Ibid., 155.

34. John Hope Franklin and Alfred A. Moss, Jr., *From Slavery to Freedom: A History of African Americans*, 8th ed., (New York: Alfred A. Knopf , 2002), 76–77.

35. Fischer, 367.

36. Talpalar, 130.

37. Fischer, 388.

38. Ibid., 227.

39. Ibid., 228.

40. Ibid., 366–368.

41. Phillips, 26.

42. Fischer, 196–197.

43. Phillips, 27.

44. Fischer, 68–72.

45. Talpalar, 211.

46. Fischer, 221–222.

47. Ibid., 253–25.

48. Franklin and Moss, 29.

49. Ibid., 29.

50. Fischer, 812.

51. Ibid., 639.

52. Phillips, 24–26.

53. Colin Woodard, *American Nations: A History of the Eleven Rival Regional Cultures of North America*, (New York: Penguin, 2011), 65.

54. Phillips, 133; Fischer, 812.

55. Fischer, 817.

56. Russell Shorto, *The Island at the Center of the World: The Epic Story of Dutch Manhattan and the Forgotten Colony that Shaped America*, (New York: Doubleday, 2004), 6.

57. Franklin and Moss, 51–52.

58. Ibid., 51.

[59.] Karl Watson, "A Brief History of Barbados," in *Barbados: Just Beyond Your Imagination*, ed. Arif Ali, (St. John's: Hansib Caribbean, 1996), 52.

[60.] Lincoln Mullen, "The Spread of U.S. Slavery, 1790–1860," interactive map, http://lincolnmullen.com/projects/slavery/, accessed Aug. 4, 2015, doi: 10.5281/zenodo.9825.

[61.] Fischer, 818.

[62.] Franklin and Moss, 71–72.

[63.] Ibid., 119–120.

[64.] Ibid., 126.

[65.] U.S. Census Bureau, 1860 Census, accessed Aug. 4, 2015, http://www.census.gov/prod/www/decennial.html.

Chapter Three

[1.] Geert Hofstede, *Cultures and Organizations: Software of Mind*, (1991; New York: McGraw-Hill, 1997), 53.

[2.] William B. Gudykunst and Stella Ting-Toomey, *Culture and Interpersonal Communication,* (Newbury Park, CA: Sage, 1988), 44.

[3.] Hofstede, 50–51.

4. Edward T. Hall, *Beyond Culture,* (Garden City: Anchor Press/Doubleday, 1976), 88, 92.

5. Hofstede, 50.

6. Ibid., 50–51.

7. Gudykunst and Ting-Toomey, 85.

8. Ibid., 85.

9. Hofstede, 50.

10. Gudykunst and Ting-Toomey, 86.

11. Hall, 103–104.

12. *The Japanese Tea Ceremony*, last modified 2011, japanese-tea-ceremony.net.

13. Harry C. Triandis, *Individualism and Collectivism,* (Boulder: Westview Press, 1995), 75.

14. William B. Gudykunst and Yuko Matsumoto, "Cross-Cultural Variability of Communication in Personal Relationships," in *Communication in Personal Relationships Across Cultures,* eds. William B. Gudykunst, Stella Ting-Toomey, and Tsukasa Nishida, (Thousand Oaks, CA: Sage, 1996), 23.

15. Hall, 98.

16. Gudykunst and Matsumoto, 31.

17. Hall, 11.

18. Gudykunst and Matsumoto, 33.

Chapter Four

1. Dan Ariely, *The (Honest) Truth About Dishonesty: How We Lie to Everyone—Especially Ourselves* (New York: Harper Collins, 2012).

2. William B. Gudykunst and Stella Ting-Toomey, *Culture and Interpersonal Communication,* (Newbury Park, CA: Sage, 1988), 44.

3. Ibid., 84.

4. Michael Carr, "Chinese 'Face' in Japanese and English (Part 1)," *The Review of Liberal Arts*, 84 (1992): 42, http://barrel.ih.otaru-uc.ac.jp/handle/10252/1737; Michael Carr, "Chinese 'Face' in Japanese and English (Part 2)," *The Review of Liberal Arts*, 85, (1993): 72, http://barrel.ih.otaru-uc.ac.jp/handle/10252/1585.

5. Gudykunst and Ting-Toomey, 85.

6. Ibid., 89.

7. Ibid., 90–91.

[8.] Stella Ting-Toomey and Leeva Chung, "Cross-Cultural Interpersonal Communication: Theoretical Trends and Research Directions," in *Communication in Personal Relationships Across Cultures,* eds. William B. Gudykunst, Stella Ting-Toomey, and Tsukasa Nishida, (Thousand Oaks, CA: Sage, 1996), 250.

[9.] Gudykunst and Ting-Toomey, 89.

[10.] Ibid., 93.

[11.] Ibid., 159.

[12.] Ibid., 93.

[13.] Ibid., 85–86.

[14.] Ibid., 85–86.

[15.] Ibid., 89–90.

[16.] Ibid., 160.

[17.] Ibid., 90.

[18.] Ibid., 160.

Chapter Five

[1.] Edward T. Hall, *Beyond Culture,* (Garden City: Anchor Press/Doubleday, 1976), 98.

2. Harry C. Triandis, *Individualism and Collectivism,* (Boulder: Westview Press, 1995), 76.

3. William B. Gudykunst and Yuko Matsumoto, "Cross-Cultural Variability of Communication in Personal Relationships," in *Communication in Personal Relationships Across Cultures,* eds. William B. Gudykunst, Stella Ting-Toomey, and Tsukasa Nishida, (Thousand Oaks, CA: Sage, 1996), 31.

4. Ibid., 32.

5. Triandis, 76.

6. Gudykunst and Matsumoto, 32.

7. Ibid., 32.

8. Ibid., 31.

9. Triandis, 32.

10. Gudykunst and Matsumoto, 31.

11. Ibid., 31.

12. Ibid., 33.

Chapter Six

1. Eva G. T. Green, Jean-Claude Deschamps, and Dario Paez, "Variation of Individualism and Collectivism

Within and Between Twenty Countries: A Typological Analysis," *Journal of Cross Cultural Psychology* 36, no. 3 (2005): 321, accessed Aug. 4, 2015, doi: 10.1177/0022022104273654; Harry C. Triandis, "The Many Dimensions of Culture," *Academy of Management Executive* 18, no. 1 (2004): 90, accessed Aug. 4. 2015, doi: 10.5465/AME.2004.12689599.

[2.] Geert Hofstede, *Cultures and Organizations: Software of Mind*, (1991; New York: McGraw-Hill, 1997), 53.

[3.] Hofstede, 50.

[4.] William B. Gudykunst and Stella Ting-Toomey, *Culture and Interpersonal Communication*, (Newbury Park, CA: Sage, 1988), 44–45.

[5.] Hofstede, 51.

[6.] Daphna Oyserman, Heather M. Coon, and Markus Kemmelmeier, "Rethinking Individualism and Collectivism: Evaluation of Theoretical Assumptions and Meta-Analyses," *Psychological Bulletin* 128, no. 1 (2002): 5, accessed Aug. 4, 2015, doi: 10.1037/0033-2909.128.1.3.

[7.] Harry C. Triandis, *Individualism and Collectivism*, (Boulder: Westview Press, 1995), 69.

[8.] Ibid., 75.

[9.] Oyserman, Coon, and Kemmelmeier, 5.

[10.] Triandis, 73.

[11.] Oyserman, Coon, and Kemmelmeier, 5.

[12.] William B. Gudykunst and Yuko Matsumoto, "Cross-Cultural Variability of Communication in Personal Relationships," in *Communication in Personal Relationships Across Cultures,* eds. William B. Gudykunst, Stella Ting-Toomey, and Tsukasa Nishida, (Thousand Oaks, CA: Sage, 1996), 23.

[13.] Oyserman, Coon, and Kemmelmeier, 5.

[14.] David Hackett Fischer, *Albion's Seed: Four British Folkways in America,* (New York: Oxford University Press, 1989), 224.

[15.] Ibid., 667–668.

[16.] Malcolm Gladwell, *Outliers: The Story of Success*, (New York: Little, Brown and Co., 2008), 166–170.

[17.] Fischer, 667.

[18.] Gudykunst and Matsumoto, 23.

[19.] Oyserman, Coon, and Kemmelmeier, 5.

[20.] Triandis, 32.

[21.] Ibid., 32.

22. Ibid., 32.

23. Hofstede, 60–61.

24. Triandis, 74; Oyserman, Coon, and Kemmelmeier, 9.

25. Theodore M. Singelis, Harry C. Triandis, Dharm P.S. Bhawuk, and Michele J. Gelfand, "Horizontal and Vertical Dimensions of Individualism and Collectivism: A Theoretical and Measurement Refinement," *Cross-Cultural Research* 29, no. 3 (1995): 244–245, accessed Aug. 4, 2015, doi: 10.1177/106939719502900302.

26. Gudykunst and Matsumoto, 24.

27. John Shelton Reed, "*The Mind of the South* and Southern Distinctiveness," *The Mind of the South: Fifty Years Later*, ed. Charles W. Eagles, (Jackson: University Press of Mississippi, 1992), 148.

28. Ibid., 146.

29. Paul C. Nagel, *The Lees of Virginia: Seven Generations of an American Family*, (New York: Oxford University Press, 1990), 266.

30. Ibid., 267.

31. Triandis, 160.

32. Triandis, 38.

Chapter Seven

[1] Harry C. Triandis, *Individualism and Collectivism*, (Boulder: Westview Press, 1995), 72–73, 129.

[2] Ibid., 72–73, 130.

[3] William B. Gudykunst and Yuko Matsumoto, "Cross-Cultural Variability of Communication in Personal Relationships," in *Communication in Personal Relationships Across Cultures*, eds. William B. Gudykunst, Stella Ting-Toomey, and Tsukasa Nishida, (Thousand Oaks, CA: Sage, 1996), p. 22.

[4] Triandis, 73.

[5] Ibid., 73.

[6] Geert Hofstede, *Cultures and Organizations: Software of Mind*, (1991; New York: McGraw-Hill, 1997), 64.

[7] Triandis, 79.

[8] Hofstede, 64.

[9] Triandis, 79.

[10] Hofstede, 64.

[11] Ibid., 67.

Chapter Eight

[1.] Geert Hofstede, *Cultures and Organizations: Software of Mind*, (1991; New York: McGraw-Hill, 1997), 50–51, 74.

[2.] Harry C. Triandis, *Individualism and Collectivism*, (Boulder: Westview Press, 1995), 57.

[3.] Ibid., 57.

[4.] Hofstede, 77.

[5.] Triandis, 58.

[6.] Hofstede, 74, 77.

[7.] William H. Frey, *Diversity Explosion: How New Racial Demographics are Remaking America*, (Washington, D.C.: Brookings Institution Press, 2015), 117.

[8.] Ibid., 119.

[9.] Ibid., 117–119.

[10.] Ibid., 119–120.

[11.] Ibid., 72.

Acknowledgments

The ideas presented in this book are built upon lifetimes of work from social scientists. I am forever grateful to those who hold the mirror up to mankind, show us who we are, and show us how we might be better. My goal in these pages has been to do the same.

This book wouldn't have been possible without Emily Blevins, who brought the kernel for it home one day, not realizing the next three years would be consumed by helping it grow. Her role as Developmental Editor has included countless hours of conversation about the ideas in the book and how best to present them. She has read more revisions than any one person should ever be asked to read, and her encouragement and support cannot be overstated. She will always be my Director of the "For Crying Out Loud, Just Plain-Talk It Department."

Editor Mark A. Bilbrey's deft hand was hugely instrumental in sharpening the quality of the language and the presentation of the ideas in the book. I asked Mark for light copy editing services and was lucky enough to receive much more: a skillful partner and keen intellect ready to apply his many abilities to the manuscript. Mark and I worked closely for the final months of editing the book, and I remain grateful for his enthusiasm and contribution to the material.

A special thanks to Carrie Sublett, who might or might not have been tricked into designing the cover of the book. (Old habits die hard, I suppose.)

Finally, an extra special thanks to the readers who helped shape the book from its early days. I'm most grateful to my friend Greg Coulter, who was willing to not only read the various versions of the book, but also to spend many hours discussing its ideas. Cassie, Liz, Philip, Donna, Mike, Grant, Lori, Brent, John: thank you.

CPSIA information can be obtained at www.ICGtesting.com
Printed in the USA
LVOW07s1051200216

475829LV00003B/1/P